GORD

Near the end of the 1968-69 professional ice hockey season, Gordie Howe, the right-wing for the Detroit Red Wings, scored the 732nd goal of his long and amazing career. His place as the greatest goal-getter in National Hockey League history is virtually assured; it seems impossible that anyone could even approach his record. In addition to holding the most goals in the NHL, he also owns the most honors. Six times he has captured the National Hockey League scoring championship. Six times he has been awarded the Hart Trophy, emblematic of the league's Most Valuable Player. Ten times he has been named to the NHL's first team of All-Stars, and in ten other seasons he was selected for the second team.

These honors and records point up what is acknowledged by most hockey experts—namely, that Gordie Howe is the finest, most talented, best all-around player in the history of the game. He is, in fact, Mr. Hockey.

This is the first full-length account of Gordie Howe's amazing career—a career that has spanned 23 years of rugged and inspired play in the world's fastest as well as fastest-growing sport.

GORDIE HOWE

by Stan Fischler

GROSSET & DUNLAP
NEW YORK

PUBLISHED SIMULTANEOUSLY IN CANADA

LIBRARY OF CONGRESS CATALOG CARD NUMBER: 76-88894

TEMPO BOOKS IS REGISTERED IN THE U.S. PATENT OFFICE

TEMPO BOOKS EDITION, 1969
FIRST PRINTING, OCTOBER 1969

PRINTED IN THE UNITED STATES OF AMERICA

Chapter One

Doing easily what others find difficult is talent; doing what is impossible for talent is genius.

—HENRI-FREDERIC AMIEL, *Journal*

THE 1966–67 National Hockey League season was in its final two weeks and the Detroit Red Wings were fighting to stave off mathematical elimination from a spot in the Stanley Cup playoffs. The Wings—then in fifth place, 10 points out of fourth, the final playoff-qualifying position—were at home in Detroit's Olympia Stadium to face the third-place Toronto Maple Leafs. A win over Toronto would keep alive Detroit's flickering hopes for a playoff berth. A loss would bar the Wings from the semi-final round of the Cup competition for the first time in five years.

In the lineup for the Wings that Sunday afternoon was Gordie Howe. He had missed the previous day's game against the Boston Bruins because of a shoulder injury and there was some doubt about his being able to go the distance against Toronto. But a sub-par Howe is better than no Howe at all, and so Detroit manager-coach Sid Abel sent Gordie and his linemates—the veteran Alex Delvecchio and the rookie Doug Roberts—out on ice for the opening face-off.

Twenty-four seconds after the puck was dropped, Howe swooped in on Terry Sawchuk, the Toronto goalie who once starred in the nets for Detroit, and banged the puck past him to give the Wings a 1–0 lead. Two minutes later Detroit scored again. And two minutes after that Howe rammed home his second goal of the game. Thus, with less than five minutes gone, the Wings led by a score of 3 to 0.

After two periods the score was 4–2, Detroit. And midway through the third period the Wings were ahead by a 5–3 margin. Then, disaster struck. Two quick Toronto goals gave the Leafs a 5–5 tie. Then, with less than three minutes to play, Toronto's Pete Stemkowski lofted the puck off the Detroit boards. The disk bounced out in front of the Detroit net and Jim Pappin back-handed the puck past a startled George Gardner and put the Leafs ahead, 6 to 5.

With two minutes left in the game, the Howe line came back on ice. Gordie, Delvecchio and Roberts launched a desperation rush, but lost the puck at the Toronto blue line. In his eagerness to retrieve the disk, Howe grabbed a Toronto player around the waist and was promptly slapped with a two-minute penalty for holding. And the Wings were dead—at least as far as the 1966–67 season was concerned.

As Howe skated to the penalty box, one would have forgiven him for an outburst of temper. He is a proud man who, despite an outward air of nonchalance, hates to lose. But there was no outburst, no display of emotion, no venting of his frustration.

He went to the penalty box with his head held high, his back ramrod straight, and the stick cradled in his hands. In other words, Gordie Howe was able to accept defeat with the same grace and style that marked his moments of victory and personal triumph. As a person, and as a professional hockey player, Gordie Howe is in a class by himself. He is, in fact, Mr. Hockey.

In effect, Detroit's season ended with the Toronto game. The Wings could have collapsed and merely gone through the motions during their final five games of the season, but with a player like Gordie Howe in the lineup, a team does not throw in the towel. And so, a few nights later against the New York Rangers, the Wings played as if they were battling for first place. They won by a score of 4 to 1, with Howe scoring the first

Detroit goal. That was his 25th of the season and gave him a career total of 714 goals.

There were immediate comparisons between Howe and Babe Ruth, who hit 714 home runs during his baseball career. There was a difference, however. Ruth's 714 home runs came in regular season play. Gordie's 714 goals had been scored in both regular season competition and high-pressure Stanley Cup games.

Sixty-five of the goals, in fact, were netted in the course of 150 Stanley Cup contests. The remaining 649 goals were chalked up in regular season games.

For Gordie Howe, goal Number 714 was but another milestone in a long and illustrious career dotted with various records, some of which may never be broken.

Five times he has captured the National Hockey League scoring championship. Six times he has been awarded the Hart Trophy, emblematic of the league's Most Valuable Player. Nine times he has been named to the NHL's first team of All-Stars, and in nine other seasons Howe has been selected for the second team of All-Stars.

He holds the record for the most goals, most assists and most points in the history of the National Hockey League. And, with Bernie (Boom-Boom) Geoffrion, ex-Montreal star and more recently with the New York Rangers, Howe shares the record for the most points in one season by a right-winger—95.

These records underline what is acknowledged by many hockey experts—namely, that Gordie Howe is the finest, most talented all-around player in the history of the National Hockey League. As Frank Selke, long-time managing director of the Montreal Canadiens, puts it: "Howe is the composite of hockey's great stars—including 'Rocket' Richard, Jean Beliveau and Milt Schmidt."

Foster Hewitt, the "voice" of the Toronto Maple Leafs and one of hockey's most respected observers, is more succinct:

"Everything you can think of in hockey," Hewitt says, "Howe is."

But beyond being regarded as the greatest player ever to pull on a uniform in the NHL, Howe also ranks as professional hockey's most durable competitor. In the bruising, brawling, frenetic sport of hockey, where most players have called it a career by age thirty-five, Howe is still going strong at the age of thirty-nine, with no thoughts of retirement, although a young superstar like Chicago's Bobby Hull often talks of quitting.

The average career span of an NHL player is 6.6 years. Gordie Howe has put in 21 years with the Red Wings. He is, in fact, the first man in league history to play 21 seasons. And, of course, he has appeared in more games than any other player in league annals. One suspects he wears an invisible sheet of armor and has a Diesel engine under his jersey.

Howe's record of durability is even more amazing when you consider that at the peak of his career he was often on the ice for up to 45 minutes of every 60-minute game. Even now Howe puts in between 20 and 25 minutes per game, sometimes more.

In his 21st season with the Wings, Gordie was still taking his regular turns at right wing. In addition, Detroit coach Sid Abel continued to use him on all power plays. And, in tight games, Howe was still helping kill penalties.

To do all of this at Howe's age exacts a great physical toll. Often, he skates to the bench in a state of near exhaustion. But he has the knack of recovering quickly, and usually within 30 seconds of hitting the bench his head is erect and he is studying the play, doping out what he might do when he takes the ice for his next turn.

For Gordie Howe is a true student of the game. Much of his success, of course, is due to his overwhelming natural ability. But much of that ability might well have been wasted on a less dedicated player. It is Howe's nature to excel at whatever he does, and to win whenever he competes.

After 21 years in the league, Howe, through a combination of instinct and experience, knows just about where his teammates and opponents are at every moment he is on the ice. What's more, he is usually able to anticipate moves before they happen. As a result, Howe is always on the move, even when he doesn't have the puck. That way he is constantly at the ready to take a pass and shoot, or set up a teammate who has a better shot at the net.

Howe, however, tends to minimize the talk about his natural instincts and abilities to anticipate a play, the way Superman might disparage his own strength.

"Anticipation," he says, "is just a fancy word for guessing. I always credit my success to the individuals I play with. It's gotta be a team effort to get goals."

Howe points out that he has often netted the puck even though he actually wasn't working hard for a goal.

"You're standing around the net and all of a sudden the puck hits your leg and goes in," he explains. "It's in the books and you'll never find out which of the 500 goals it was. It's like a blooper in baseball. It looks like a line drive in the box score the next day."

Howe believes that scoring goals is a combination of luck and hard work.

"If you work real hard," he says, "the luck will come with you. That's my ambition, to keep luck on my side; so I'm going to continue working as hard as I can."

Howe then sums up his overall approach to the game this way:

"The danger zone is around the center of the ice, just inside the opposing blue line. That's where they can really hit you. About that point the defense is often staggered. By that I mean that one defenseman is playing a little further back than the other. If you get by one, the other one is waiting for you, lining you up as you cut across the blue line.

"By the time you get to the blue line, the forwards are usually back too. A guy will hit the blue line, make a pass, then pause to look at the pass and admire how well it was done. At the same time he is cutting in toward the net. Or a guy will shoot and do the same thing. He's busy watching, admiring his fine shot when, bang, along comes the check from the side. Marcel Pronovost has been one of the best at catching a man looking down or away in that area.

"I tell the fellows to make their play and not pause to admire it. If it was so good," Howe remarks with just the trace of a smile, "they'll be able to read about it in the papers the next day."

It is obvious, then, that Howe is not the type to be caught napping on ice. Yet, someone watching big "Number 9" for the first time is apt to think that Howe is loafing. Even Maurice "Rocket" Richard, whose scoring records have been shattered by Howe, once complained that "Gordie would be even greater if he approached his job with a little more enthusiasm."

Richard's mild criticism is understandable. He skated with verve and dash, and on ice his style was not unlike a bomb ready to explode at any moment. But that just happened to be Richard's way. It is not Gordie Howe's way. His moves on ice are economical, almost lazy, and there are what appear to be faster skaters in the NHL, but who simply use more energy and moves. Howe moves with the grace of a Joe DiMaggio loping after a fly ball that you knew he could not possibly catch —until he did. And Howe, with his long strides, covers as much if not more of the ice than most of his teammates or competitors.

Outwardly, then, Howe is relaxed, cool and in control. Inwardly, he is the same. Jack Adams, who coached the Wings when Howe joined them, describes Gordie's attitude by saying:

"In the dressing room before a big game he was always just as cool as he was on the ice. Why, no matter what the pressure, he could pass a cup of tea on a stick across to another player and not shake a bit. He was a cool article all right."

Then Adams recalled one specific clutch game when Howe had the puck right in front of the net and was toying with the goaltender.

"I'm hollering, 'Shoot! Shoot!, Gordie,' " Adams explained. "It's late in the game and the score is tied. Finally, he slips the puck in and we win. When he comes back to the bench I say, 'For God's sake, Gordie, what were you waiting for?' He says in that drawl of his, 'Aw, Jack, I knew I had him. I just wanted him to make the first move. I just wanted to be sure."

Coach Sid Abel agrees completely with Adams' analysis.

"I remember sitting next to Gordie in overtime playoff games," Abel says. "The situation was tense but Gordie would tell some story about something that happened during his kid days out West. His mind was a thousand miles away, though he was actually paying attention to the game in a detached sort of way. Gordie doesn't wear himself out worrying about what's happening on the ice. He studies the action, yes. But he doesn't worry about it."

Howe also strikes a relaxed pose on the ice at times to lull an opponent into a sense of false security. Once lulled, the defender lets up just long enough for Gordie to get off or receive a pass, or fire a bullet-like shot at the net.

The fact that Howe has conserved himself, both physically and mentally, no doubt is one of the main reasons that he has endured for so long a time in the NHL, much to the chagrin of the other teams which must play the Wings and Gordie Howe during the season. For the last few years, NHL goalies have been expressing the same sentiment once voiced by Chicago's All-Star netminder, Glenn Hall.

"For my sake," said Hall, "I hope that Howe quits tomorrow. He can beat you from any angle." Then Hall went on to recall how he had once stopped Howe on a break-away. "I was feeling pretty good about that," Hall continued. "But as he was going by, he rapped the rebound right out of the air and into the net."

Another reason Howe has survived in the NHL for 21 seasons is his enormous strength. He stands an even six feet tall and weighs 204 pounds, which makes him one of the heaviest players in the league.

Off ice and in street clothes, however, he looks deceptively slim, particularly so because of his long neck, narrow face and long arms. Add to these physical characteristics his graying hair and pleasant open face, and Gordie Howe, in mufti, appears more like a business executive than a hockey player.

But on closer inspection you notice the slope of his shoulders. They are well-developed and well-muscled, but rise into his neck at an angle of forty-five degrees. Which once led Howe's former teammate, Larry Jeffrey, to crack: "Gordie, you're the only guy in the world who keeps a permanent hanger in his suits to fill out the shoulders."

Still, they are the shoulders of an athlete. And Howe's face is the face of a hockey player long at the hockey wars. In the course of his career, Howe has picked up close to 400 stitches in his face, and also has suffered the loss of a dozen teeth.

"I had 50 stitches in my face one year," Howe remarks in a professional tone, sounding almost like a gas station attendant discussing the number of gallons pumped in one day. "Another season I only had 10 stitches. That was a good year."

In addition, Howe has sustained damage to the cartilages in both knees, broken ribs, a broken wrist, several broken toes, a dislocated shoulder, an ankle injury, a variety of head cuts, and a severe skull fracture during the Stanley Cup playoffs of 1950 that nearly ended his life.

Howe dismissed his assorted injuries with a shrug and a casual, "Aw, it's not all that bad."

And, in truth, Howe has been most fortunate in that he has missed very little ice time because of injury. In 21 campaigns, Howe has missed just 42 regular season games. Of course, some games were played despite injuries that might have sent a less dedicated man to the bench.

Chapter Two

ANOTHER of the reasons Howe has suffered fewer broken bones than most NHL players is because the majority of his competitors are inclined to give Gordie a wide berth, rather than risk a direct clash with him. For among the players on the league's five other teams, Howe is regarded as one of the roughest—if not *the* roughest—of opponents.

Howe has never led the NHL in penalties, but has always been among the leaders, year in and year out. And it is the opinion of many players that Howe escapes more trips to the penalty box only because he is a past master at escaping detection.

"He's always on the outer edge of the rulebook," charges Eric Nesterenko of the Chicago

Black Hawks. "You never know when he's going to slip over into what's dirty."

Ted Lindsay, who played with Howe for 13 years, and against him for three more as a member of the Black Hawks, contends that "Gordie gets away with more than anyone else in hockey."

And back in 1960, Andy Bathgate, then a member of the Rangers but recently a teammate of Howe's at Detroit, wrote an article for a national magazine in which he accused Howe of deliberately inflicting head cuts, and intentionally shooting the puck at the heads of some opponents.

Carl Brewer, at one time an All-Star defenseman for the Toronto Maple Leafs, recalls an incident involving Howe and himself. As Brewer describes it, he and Howe fell in a tangle behind the Toronto net just as the play was whistled dead. Brewer was on top and Howe called out, "Okay, okay, Carl, play's over." Brewer resisted the temptation to give Howe a quick jab in the clinch and both players got up.

Later in the period, Howe and Brewer again wound up in a tangle, this time with Gordie on top. When the whistle blew, Brewer relaxed, figuring Howe would return the courtesy extended earlier. Instead, Howe gave Brewer a poke in the ribs.

On the other hand, Montreal goalie Gump Worsley probably owes his continued presence in the NHL to Howe. It was during a game at Madison Square Garden when Worsley was tending goal for the New York Rangers. Worsley flopped to the ice making a save and the puck dribbled loose in front of his unprotected face as Howe swooped in.

Another player might have wound up and shot, inflicting serious injury on Worsley in thc process. Instead, Howe held back and set himself up as a screen in front of Worsley until Gump could smother the puck.

As Worsley arose, he said to Howe, "Thanks, bud." Howe replied: "Before I'm through, I'm going to score a few more and you're going to stop me a few more. So we're about even."

So, take your choice. Either Howe is rough or dirty, or a prince. But to other players in the NHL, it really doesn't make much difference. Violence is an integral part of hockey, and Howe excels at all facets of the game, including the violence. What's more, Howe has to be tough, for the simple reason that he is the most hounded, closely checked player in the league. He cannot allow himself to be intimidated.

"When you go up against Howe you're a little scared," Nesterenko admits. "But you admire him for the way he can keep you off. It's your job to stay with him and keep him under control, but unless you keep thinking about it all the time, you're inclined to stay a step or so away from him."

In addition to his strength, Howe also has the ability to fight, and fight exceptionally well. One-time NHL referee Red Storey claims that if Howe had gone into professional boxing, he could have been the world's heavyweight champion. The few NHL players who have tangled fistically with Howe would support Storey's contention.

Perhaps Howe's most famous on-ice brawl was his battle with Lou Fontinato. It took place at Madison Square Garden during the 1958–59 season while Fontinato was playing defense for the Rangers.

Actually, the initial spark was ignited between Howe and Eddie Shack, now of the Boston Bruins. Ranger coach Phil Watson had assigned Shack to shadow Howe during the first several Ranger–Red Wing games of the 1958–59 campaign and Shack had done a comparatively good job of containing Gordie. But on this particular night at the Garden, Shack came out of a tangle with Howe sporting a cut that took three stitches to close.

As Shack quarreled behind the net with Gordie, Fontinato zeroed in on Howe and smashed him into the boards. Both dropped their gloves and Louie went in low at Howe, firing the initial punches. Gordie used his left hand to grab Fontinato's sweater, and then drove his right fist into Louie's nose. Fontinato crumpled to the ice, his nose broken.

"There was nothing I could do but fight," Howe said later in a typical understatement.

A Detroit teammate related in somewhat awed tones: "Howe's punches went whop-whop-whop—just like someone chopping wood."

Fontinato went to a nearby hospital to have the nose set, and though he had taken a good going over, he was still full of fight. "Howe needn't think he's Jack Dempsey just because he put me here," Fontinato snapped. Howe had a mild rejoinder: "I came to play hockey," he said, "not to fight."

In the wake of the brawl, Howe scored two goals, but the Wings still lost to the Rangers by a score of 5 to 4. The Wings finished sixth that season and the Rangers wound up fifth. New York had been expected to finish higher, but the club lost its last five games and ended up a point behind fourth-place Toronto.

Watson always felt that what cooked the Rangers that year was a pair of photographs published by Life magazine. One photo showed Howe in the dressing room after the fight, looking cool and calm, and bearing no marks of combat. The other photo showed Fontinato with swollen eyes and his nose encased in bandages. As Watson said later: "When the guys on the club saw those pictures, the heart just went out of them."

In hockey, nice guys may not always finish last, but it's the tough guys who usually finish first.

The sport of hockey also has other rules of conduct, however. One of them is that a player does not hold a grudge. And so, a few months after being pounded by Howe, Fontinato and Gordie met at a dinner in Canada. A mutual friend was in the middle and said to Louie: "I guess you know Gordie Howe." Fontinato replied, "I guess so, but I'm not sure I should lower my hands to shake with him." Then Louie smiled and the pair shook hands.

Howe's liberal use of his elbows while on the ice also has earned him a nickname among his colleagues—"The Wiper." King Clancy of the Toronto Maple Leafs once explained why Howe was so tagged.

"Have you ever watched anybody try to scrape ice off a windshield?" Clancy asked. "Well, that's Gordie and those elbows."

Toronto defenseman Allan Stanley recalled running into Howe's elbow some years ago. He emerged with a broken nose.

"Funny thing," Stanley added, "I got the penalty on the play."

So, among hockey players, Howe is admired if not beloved. But among hockey fans, Howe is both admired and, well, beloved.

In Detroit, Howe is "Mister Sports." Wherever and whenever he appears in public, he is besieged by the young and old alike. Some merely want his autograph. Others offer all sorts of advice on how to play the game of hockey. And there are a few—especially in the other NHL cities—who enjoy giving Howe a deft needle.

On Howe's part, he more than tolerates these fans. He thoroughly enjoys their company. On the night he scored his 545th goal and broke Rocket Richard's career scoring mark, for example, Howe spent an hour after the game patiently signing his name to hundreds of pieces of paper. Usually, Howe includes a personal message with his signature. He might write "Best of everything, Gordie Howe"; or, "Best wishes, Gordie Howe."

If a fan tries to prolong the conversation, Gordie will oblige, often with a quip; such as the time a girl in her twenties asked Howe for his autograph, and then added: "I'm from Newfoundland." Gordie smiled and replied, "Awww, don't feel bad about it."

Like many Canadians, Howe punctuates his sentences with an all-inclusive "Awww" or "Ay." When a question requires a long explanation, he'll draw out his words—like "awwfulllll"—to give himself a chance to phrase it correctly. Sometimes he drags them out so long that he appears to stammer. But he is sharp with a comeback.

During Detroit's miserable 1966–67 season, for example, Howe was standing in the lobby of Montreal's Queen Elizabeth Hotel when a fan approached and needled, "Canadiens beat you bad last week."

"Heck," Gordie shot back, "You know hockey. Hockey is a game of mistakes. Our mistake was getting out of bed that morning."

If he so wished, Howe could be a "showboat." But that is not his style, although there have been occasions when he allowed himself just a touch of flamboyancy. Once, during a game at Toronto, he skated over to the photographers' cage at the side of the rink and shouted: "Get set and I'll pop one." Two minutes later he deposited the puck in the Toronto net. It was no less significant than Babe Ruth's "called" home run in the 1932 World Series.

Another time, again at Maple Leaf Gardens, a

fan in a rinkside seat was taunting Howe unmercifully. Gordie bided his time until there was a face-off in the vicinity of the obnoxious spectator. Then he neatly shoveled some ice shavings onto the blade of his stick and, with a flick of his wrist, dropped the shavings on the man's homburg.

Normally, however, Howe is self-effacing, almost humble. He is quick to compliment his fellow players. "I think [Bobby] Hull and [Frank] Mahovlich are a couple of real fine hockey players," Howe has remarked. "Jean Beliveau already proved himself great. But I think Hull is the guy who can get my record, pass me, Richard and everybody else." There are those, however, who believe that Hull—a completely "new school" player—is less dedicated to the game of hockey than Howe and more apt to retire prematurely.

There are similarities between Hull and Howe. In the NHL today, only Hull's shot comes close in speed to Howe's—which has been clocked at a little better than 120 miles an hour. Gordie can get off a shot at maximum velocity simply by raising his stick a foot or so, then actually flicking his wrists. Hull usually raises his stick three or four feet and then slaps the puck in order to achieve maximum velocity.

Hull also can switch hands and he is now at the point where his unnatural left-handed shot is almost as hard to handle as his natural right-handed shot. The difference is that Howe shooting left-handed is as difficult to handle as Howe shooting right-handed.

Amazingly enough, Howe sees nothing at all unusual in his being ambidextrous. Once, when he was asked about his unique talent, Howe turned to his former teammate, Parker MacDonald, and said, "Anybody could do that. You could do that, couldn't you, Parker?"

MacDonald laughed. "Not me," he answered. "I couldn't do it in a million years." Later, MacDonald said, "That's Gordie Howe for you. He doesn't realize he can do things that other players can't even try to do."

Chapter Three

HIS GIVEN name is Gordon Howe and he was born March 31st, 1928, in Floral, Saskatchewan, a town on the outskirts of Saskatoon, in the heart of Canada's wheat belt. Gordie was the fourth of nine children and when he was three months old the Howe family moved from a farm in Floral to a two-story clapboard house on Avenue L North in Saskatoon. Today, Saskatoon has a population of approximately 100,000. When Gordie Howe was growing up there, the population was about half as much as it is now. It has always been a friendly city, and a quiet city. And, of course, it has always been a hockey city.

"I believe Gordie got his first pair of skates when he was about six," his mother, Catherine, recalls. "A lady came to the door with a bag of clothes she was selling for fifty cents. I bought them, and Gordie jumped into the bag right away. He pulled out a pair of skates. They were much too big for him, but I remember he got four or five pairs of wool socks and got the skates on that way. From then on it seemed he was always wrapped up in hockey somehow. If he wasn't playing he was collecting syrup labels so he could get hockey cards. He got hundreds of them. We still have them put away upstairs someplace."

Howe's father, Albert, remembers Gordie as a "big . . . awkward kid . . . always so much bigger than the others . . . and always very shy." And Mrs. Howe adds: "Yes, he was always clumsy as a boy. And he was a quiet boy. The kids, because he was so big and clumsy, used to call him 'doughhead.' Oh, how that used to make me angry. You know it means stupid, or someone who doesn't know anything. It used to bother him, but he'd never fight with the kids because he always seemed so conscious he was so much bigger than they were."

Howe's formal education ended after eight years of elementary school. "He failed two times in the third grade," his mother recalls with the clarity of a mother who remembers her son's setbacks as well as his triumphs. "He wasn't bad in school. He always tried. But the second time he failed, it took the heart right out of him. I remember seeing him coming down the street crying.

"I said, 'Sit down, Gordie, tell me what's wrong. Is the work too difficult? Don't you understand the teacher? Do you ask her questions about what you don't understand?' He said, 'No, ma, I don't want to bother her.' And then we both had a good, long cry."

For Gordie Howe, then, perhaps hockey was a way to escape the cruelties and harsh realities of life. Or perhaps he was just born to hockey greatness. At any rate, from the time he got hold of his first pair of skates, hockey has been Gordie Howe's way of life.

He got his first hockey stick from Ab Welsh, who had been a forward on the old Saskatoon Quakers. "I was nine years old when I got that first stick," Howe says. "He never gave one to the other kids. He saved his broken sticks or the ones whose lie he didn't like for me. He used a Number 7 lie. That's probably why I use a Number 7 lie now. I watched him and I studied his style. He was strictly a position player. I never heard an unkind word said about him. He's still my favorite. The first one is always the best."

Once he had a stick in his hands, Howe never let go.

"Any time of the year, any time of the day, you'd see him with a stick in his hands," Gordie's father recalls. "He'd walk along, swatting at clumps of dirt or stones. Once, one summer, I came home from work, and there's Gordie firing pucks at a barrel that was up against the side of the house. Shingles were all over the ground. I had to put my foot down on that."

His father also remembers that Gordie was turned down the first time he tried to join one of Saskatoon's midget teams. "And I told him never to take dirt from nobody. Because if you do, they'll keep throwing it on you."

Well, perhaps Howe has taken some dirt along the way to hockey greatness. But if so, it never robbed him of his determination to succeed. Mrs. Bert Hodges, who managed Howe when he was a member of the King George Athletic Club's midget team, says of him:

"Gordie Howe was always out there after dark. He knew what he wanted and he got it. It could be the coldest night of the year, and Gordie would be out there practicing by himself."

He started out as a goalie, probably because he was deemed too big and awkward to skate as a forward or a defenseman. Playing between the pipes held no great attraction for Howe. Years later, he was to say: "I was a goalie for a couple of seasons as a kid and that was enough." Then, smiling, he added:

"Since playing in the National Hockey League I remember a game against the Toronto Maple Leafs in which I made a heck of a save on Frank Mahovlich. It was the year he scored 36 goals [1962–63] and we were trailing by a goal so we pulled Roger Crozier [the Detroit goalie] in the final minute. Mahovlich got loose and I got back in the net just in time to catch his shot on my elbow. I'm still bragging about the save. But I told Crozier he didn't have to worry. I sure don't want his job."

Howe believes that his days as a kid goaltender—holding his stick with one hand—is one of the reasons he can switch hands and shoot from either side. He also remembers kicking out shots with "shin pads" that consisted of magazines and mail-order catalogues stuck in his socks. And he recalls vividly the icy winters in Saskatoon.

"I guess the coldest would be 50 degrees below zero. A lot of times it would be 25 degrees below. When I played goalie, I remember I used to skate a mile from my house to the rink, holding the pads up in front of me to cut the wind. At one rink they had a heated shack and a guy would ring a cowbell and the forward lines and defense for both teams would go off and sit in the shack by the pot-bellied stove and warm up while the alternates played."

Howe was a goalie for two years. Then, at the age of eleven, he was shifted to right wing. Meanwhile, he kept growing. In the summers, Gordie worked for a construction company, lugging 85-pound bags of cement. He also worked on farms around Saskatoon, putting in 12-hour days, eating five big meals daily. At age fifteen, Howe weighed 200 pounds and was heavily muscled. Despite his bulk, he was no longer awkward—at least not while playing hockey. On the ice he was quick, graceful and assured. And so it was no surprise to the hockey buffs of Saskatoon when Fred McCorry, a scout for the New York Rangers, tapped Gordie for the Rangers' training camp at Winnipeg the summer that Gordie was fifteen.

He arrived in the Rangers' camp carrying a small bag that contained a shirt, a set of underwear, a toothbrush, and his skates. For a young man with an outgoing personality, a sudden introduction to the National Hockey League at the tender age of fifteen would have been a frightening experience. But to a shy, introverted teenager such as Gordie Howe was at the time, the experience was close to shattering.

At the training table, for example, an older "pro" kept taking Gordie's plate. He was near the point of starvation when another veteran pro, defenseman Alf Pike, noticed what was going on. "Hey," he called to the plate swiper, "drop that and let the kid eat." Pike later became coach of the Rangers, but eventually was fired because of his easy-going nature.

There were other embarrassments for Howe in the Rangers' camp as well. For one, he did not know how to put on his equipment.

"I just dropped the gear on the floor in front of me and watched the others," Gordie remembers. "I found out pretty early that the best way to learn was to keep my mouth shut and my eyes open."

But the others noticed Howe's equipment problem and teased him about it. Howe stuck it out, however, until his roommate was injured and sent home. Lonely and homesick himself, Howe fled back to Saskatoon a few days later. That winter, a scout for the Red Wings, Fred Pinckney, spotted Howe, and the following summer Gordie was invited to the Detroit training camp at Windsor, Ontario. The Detroit boss at the time was Jack Adams alias "Jolly Jawn," a tough hombre who could melt steel with a searing monologue, but who had an unfailing eye for hockey talent.

"There was this day in Windsor and it was the

first day I ever saw him," Adams says. "He was a big, rangy youngster who skated so easily and always seemed so perfectly balanced. It tickled me to watch him. So I called him over to the boards and said, 'What's your name, son?' A lot of kids that age choke up when they start talking to you. But he just looked me in the eye and said real easy like, 'My name's Howe.' I then remember saying, 'If you practice hard enough and try hard enough, maybe you'll make good someday.' "

Detroit signed Howe to a contract that called for a $4,000 bonus. About an hour or so after the signing Adams found Howe standing in the hallway outside his office. He looked heartsick. "What's the matter?" Adams asked. "Well," Gordie replied, "you promised me a Red Wing jacket but I don't have it yet." Howe got his jacket.

But then he ran into another problem, this one more serious. The Red Wings had assigned Howe to their Junior "A" amateur farm team in Galt, Ontario. Because Howe was from a western city, and because Galt was in the eastern part of Canada, his transfer to the Galt club was ruled illegal. And so, for his first year in organized hockey, Howe was allowed on ice only for practice sessions and exhibition games.

Under those circumstances, Gordie's shyness

again came to the surface and for a time it appeared that Detroit would lose its bright young prospect, just as the Rangers had. The Red Wings, however, acted where the Rangers had not. They enrolled Gordie in the Galt Collegiate Institute and Vocational School. Never much of a student, Gordie dropped out after a couple of classes. But at least the Wings had tried to help. And for that he was grateful.

The next year, which was 1945, Howe was assigned by Detroit to its Omaha team in the U. S. Hockey League. Almost immediately, Gordie made it big, scoring 22 goals and adding 26 assists for the season. Ott Heller, who had played and starred with the Rangers before dropping down to the U.S.H.L., says of his first encounter with Howe: "I got the kid in the corner, but I didn't have him there for long. I thought I had a bag full of wildcats."

Within a few weeks of Howe's debut with Omaha, fans were lined up outside the dressing room door, waiting for his autograph. Sometimes he went through what was for him the ordeal of meeting the fans face-to-face and affixing his signature to the pieces of paper which they held before him like so many offerings. Other times he just couldn't go through with it. On those occasions he would flee through the dressing room window.

Gordie remembers his fast exits. He also recalls Omaha's first road swing.

"We were in Minneapolis, and at about four thirty I went downstairs in the hotel to eat. Some of the guys were already eating there, but I looked at that dining room and it looked so big and nice that I didn't want to go in. I went around the corner to a drugstore and had a milkshake." Then he smiles and adds: "I got two goals on that milkshake and we beat them, 3 to 1."

To help Gordie conquer his shyness, Red Wing officials assigned him a cocky and aggressive roommate named Ted Lindsay. Howe and Lindsay hit it off immediately. In years to come, they, along with Sid Abel, would form one of the most-feared and productive lines in the history of the National Hockey League.

Often, the three of them would make it look terribly easy. But, of course, it was not. In their early years with Detroit, for example, Howe and Lindsay often practiced together when the regular workout was over. In the course of one of those extra-curricular sessions, they discovered that the puck would bounce out in front of the goal if shot into the other team's corner at a certain angle. Naturally, they told Abel about the discovery, but it was essentially their play and the two of them worked on it for hours until it was perfected. The first time Howe and Lindsay used the play during a game it resulted in a goal. For the next two seasons, Lindsay scored on perhaps two dozen breakaways by skating straight at the goal while Howe shot the puck into that special corner. After two seasons, the other teams in the league figured out what Howe and Lindsay were doing. The Lindsay "breakaways" became less frequent, and eventually the other clubs copied the Howe-Lindsay specialty. Now, the play is standard for NHL teams, and normally it is employed on home ice.

Lindsay, now retired, ranks as one of the highest goal scorers in NHL history. An articulate, candid fellow, Lindsay helped Howe get over at least some of his initial shyness. Gordie himself has acquired a great deal of polish over the years.

"It took a while for the shyness to wear off," he admits. "I think what helped was the way I improved on ice. As I became sure of myself as a player I felt better with the fans. I think the turning point came about 1954. Some of the other players and myself did public relations work for a brewery. I had to go out and meet people. After the first few times I got more at ease. Soon I realized that I had an obligation to the fans."

Now, Howe ducks no one. Not only will he stand around and sign autographs and trade banter with the fans, but he goes so far as to say: "The only thing that bothers me now is when somebody won't come up to me. They'll stand sorta far away and say, 'Look, there goes the big shot.'" Then he slowly drawls, "Heck, I'm no big shot."

Chapter Four

WHEN Gordie Howe joined the Red Wings for the 1946–47 season, having been promoted from Omaha, the dominant teams in the National Hockey League were the Montreal Canadiens and the Toronto Maple Leafs. The dominant player was Montreal's "Rocket" Richard. The 1940s, in fact, could be called the "Richard Era," just as the 1950s were the "Howe Era," and the 1960s are the "Hull Era." Richard, incidentally, wore number nine on his jersey. Except for his first season with the Wings, Howe also has worn number nine. During that first season with Detroit, Howe wore number 17. He grabbed nine when it became available because in those days hockey teams travelled by train, and lower berths were assigned to the players with low numbers. Bobby Hull also wears number nine on his jersey, although he sported number 16 during his first six seasons with the Chicago Black Hawks. There was undoubtedly more than coincidence involved in Hull's switch of numbers.

At any rate, Hull is on record as having called Howe the greatest of all hockey players, and he adds: "I've always looked up to Gordie as one I'd like to be half as good as." Howe, of course, has a great deal of respect for Bobby's talents, although he once pointed out: "Hull showed too much admiration for the established stars when he first came up. He shied away from hitting them, not because he was afraid, but because of respect."

That was not one of Howe's shortcomings. On Detroit's first road trip during his rookie season, Howe collided with Richard during a game at the Montreal Forum. Richard swung. Howe ducked, then swung at Richard and caught him flush on the jaw. The Rocket toppled to the ice, but arose within a few seconds, more embarrassed than hurt. But as he got up, Richard heard Abel shout at him: "That'll teach you not to fool with our rookies, you phony Frenchman." Richard promptly skated over to Abel, threw a punch, and broke Abel's nose in three places.

It would be nice—but inaccurate—to say that Howe achieved instant stardom. He did not.

True, Howe did score a goal in his first NHL game, beating Turk Broda of the Maple Leafs. The date was October 16, 1946. "The puck was lying loose ten feet from the net," Howe says of his first goal. "I just slapped it in." He retrieved the puck, took it home and gave it to his family. "But I have no idea what happened to it," Howe relates. "The trouble with those things is that they lose their importance." But he notched only six more goals that season and added 15 assists for a total of 22 points.

And yet, even as an unseasoned rookie of eighteen, Howe betrayed flashes of brilliance that marked him for future greatness. There was, for example, the game against Boston in which Howe outfoxed the veteran, All-Star defenseman Dit Clapper, whose NHL longevity record was later broken by Howe. As Clapper went to check him, Howe changed hands on his stick and, with his body between Clapper and the puck, got off a clean shot on net. "I think," Ted Lindsay has remarked, "that that's when Dit decided he'd quit hockey."

"What helps you on stick handling," Howe says, "is that when you're a kid, you play with a tennis ball. There was a family in Saskatoon that had a rink with sideboards between the house and the barn. We'd go all day there with a tennis ball, 15 guys to a side, and when the ball got frozen we'd go over and knock on the window of the house. The lady would open the window and we'd throw in the frozen ball and she'd throw out the other one. That way," Howe continues, "you learn to stick handle and pass without looking at the puck or where you're going to pass it. If you kept your eyes on the puck you'd end up in the rafters. You take glances at it, but you know it's there by the feel."

Detroit finished fourth during Howe's rookie season and lost in five games to Toronto in the first round of the Stanley Cup playoffs. Against the Maple Leafs, Howe failed to pick up either a goal or an assist, but he did accumulate 18 minutes in penalties, battling continually with Toronto rookie Howie Meeker and assorted other Leafs.

Gordie showed a marked improvement during his second season with the Wings. He netted 16 goals and added 28 assists for a total of 44 points in 60 games. The Red Wings wound up in second place but bowed to the Maple Leafs in the finals of the Stanley Cup competition.

The following year, Howe missed 20 games because of a torn cartilage in his right knee. The fact that the torn cartilage was one of the few injuries he has sustained is also part of the amazing Gordie Howe story.

Hockey, like football, is basically a contact sport. Of the two, hockey is probably the more dangerous, simply because NHL players skate at speeds up to 25 miles an hour. When two players collide on ice, chances are that one, and sometimes both, will suffer an injury ranging anywhere from a minor cut to a fractured skull.

The hard rubber puck also poses a danger, particularly when it comes off a stick at 100 miles an hour. Skates, too, can cause injuries, especially during pile-ups in front of the net, when seven or eight players may be fighting for the disk. And sticks, of course, can become lethal weapons, sometimes intentionally and sometimes not.

A few years ago, for example, Detroit's All-Star defenseman, Doug Barkley, lost an eye after being hit by the sharp edge of a stick blade. In that instance, Barkley was the victim of an unfortunate accident. In the 1950 Stanley Cup playoffs, Howe was to suffer an unfortunate and near-fatal accident. But aside from that, he has been relatively free of disabling injury. There are reasons: his brute strength, his magnificent reflexes, and his great instinct for avoiding dangerous situations before they develop. Another, and perhaps more important, reason is Howe's habit of keeping himself in top condition during the off-season as well as in season. He does not smoke, for instance, and never has.

"Early in my career," Howe explains, "my coach told me it wouldn't do me any good to smoke cigarettes, so I never tried them. All I know is that when I see a boy smoking I know he's either a little shot trying to be a big shot, or he's gone over to the social side and doesn't want to be a hockey player."

Of all the injuries suffered by Howe, the most bizarre occurred at the Montreal Forum in 1961. There was a face-off in the Detroit end and Howe was the Red Wing involved in it. Just before the puck was dropped, defenseman Marcel Pronovost skated over to Howe and asked him to step aside when the puck went down on ice. Pronovost wanted a clear shot at a Montreal player who had dealt him a stiff check a few minutes earlier. Howe did as he was asked, but the play got fouled up and Gordie shifted himself right into the line of fire. Pronovost missed his target and slammed full tilt into Howe. Gordie ended up with a broken shoulder and missed six games.

"Naturally, I felt pretty bad about it," Pronovost says in relating the incident. "But all Gordie said in the first-aid room was, 'Marcel, you're a rotten body checker. You better get your eyes tested.' "

Following surgery to repair the damaged cartilage in his right knee, Howe appeared in 40 games during the 1948–49 campaign. He netted 12 goals, added 25 assists, and was selected for the second team of All-Stars. It was a creditable performance for a third-year man, especially when the man in question was only twenty-one and coming back after knee surgery.

Yet, there was a nagging suspicion among some Detroit fans, and some players around the league for that matter, that perhaps Howe had been over-rated, that perhaps he had matured too early and had reached his peak as a teen-ager. After all, 35 goals in three seasons was hardly anything to write home about. Certainly he continued to show those flashes of brilliance, but at the same time he had failed to correct two major faults which had marked his formative years in the National Hockey League.

One was his irritating tendency to misuse his talents for the sake of showmanship. Sid Abel recalls that "Gordie would come in and stick-handle around a defenseman . . . then he'd swing back and stick-handle around the same defenseman again, beating him a different way. I guess he just wanted to show that the first time was no fluke."

His second major fault was a tendency to draw too many needless penalties. It is one thing not to be intimidated by opponents. It is another to go looking for fights. Which is exactly what Howe was doing during his first three seasons in the league. Finally, Jack Adams took Howe aside and snapped at him: "What do you think you have to do, Howe, beat up the whole league player by player? Now settle down and play some hockey."

Howe got the message, just in time for the Stanley Cup playoffs. Detroit had finished atop the league and had little trouble beating the Canadiens in the opening round. But in the finals against Toronto, the Wings came out second best. The Detroit setback was no fault of Howe's. Gordie, in fact, emerged as the star of the Stanley Cup competition by scoring eight goals and adding three assists in 11 games, which was tops in goals and points. Recalling that performance, Howe says with a grin:

"I still wasn't so sure I was a star, because one day, back home in Saskatoon, a kid came up and asked for my autograph. While I signed it he said, 'Mr. Howe, what do you do in the winter?' "

But, of course, he was a star. His over-all performance against Montreal and Toronto in the playoffs had pushed Howe over the thin line that divides the good players from the great players.

The following season (1949–50) Howe scored 35 goals—matching his total for the three previous years—and added 33 assists, for a point total of 68. For the second consecutive season he was voted to the second team of All-Stars, again finishing behind Rocket Richard in the voting for the right-wing position. More importantly, Howe was the league's third highest scorer. Only his linemates, Lindsay and Abel, compiled higher point totals.

The Howe-Lindsay-Abel "Production Line" had become one of the best in the history of professional hockey, and Howe, more mature and confident, blended in perfectly. For hockey fans of that era, there were few greater thrills than watching Howe, Lindsay and Abel on a rush into enemy ice. The Production Line helped Detroit to a first-place finish that year and the Wings were favored to win the Stanley Cup. No one realized it at the time, but the Red Wings were embarking on a period of success all but unmatched in National Hockey League history.

It was at that point—at the start of the semifinal round—that Gordie Howe was struck down, nearly for life.

Chapter Five

THERE WAS an air of optimism around Detroit's Olympia Arena on March 28, 1950, as the Red Wings prepared for the opening round against the Toronto Maple Leafs. Detroit had finished the regular season's schedule 14 points ahead of third-place Toronto. Jack Adams, general manager of the Red Wings, frankly told reporters: "There'll be no alibis if we don't take the Cup. Barring injuries, we have the team we think can take it."

But the Red Wings were confronted with two very significant obstacles, both mental. They realized that the Maple Leafs had won the Stanley Cup for three consecutive seasons, the last time with a fourth-place club. Furthermore, the Leafs had won 11 straight playoff games from Detroit and had knocked the Wings out of the running for three straight seasons.

When someone remarked to Leaf coach Hap Day that the Wings appeared more worried over the outcome of the series than the high-spirited Leafs, Day said with a wry smile: "That's the trouble."

On the eve of the opening game, headlines in the Toronto *Globe and Mail* pretty well summed up the feelings in the respective camps: LEAF BOSS PRESCRIBES HARD, HONEST TOIL FOR CUP RETENTION . . . WINGS FEEL LEAF JINX HAS RUN ITS COURSE.

The bitterness that flamed among the players on the opposing teams was no better reflected than by Ted Lindsay. "This is our profession," he remarked. "It's a game you get paid for—but when it comes to the Leafs, we'd play them for nothing."

Referee George Gravel, the bald-pated French-Canadian, knew he had an unusually difficult game on his hands when he skated out to center ice. Gravel possessed a rare sense of humor and the first thing he did upon reaching the face-off circle was to bow from the waist in the direction of the press box. He was greeted with scattered boos, and then he lined up the teams for the opening face-off.

But Gravel's humor failed to infect the antagonists. In the first period Marty Pavelich and Fleming Mackell slugged it out. The Wings' Pavelich bloodied Mackell's nose and both received major penalties. Later, Bill Juzda, the tank-like Leaf defenseman, and Howe swung freely at each other and both were sent off the ice with major penalties.

Neither team scored in the first period, but after ten seconds of the second, Max Bentley of the Leafs outdrew Max McNab and got the puck to Bill Barilko. The huge defenseman saw Joe Klukay scooting to the right side. Klukay called for a pass, got it, and flipped a back-hander past Detroit goalie Harry Lumley.

Additional goals by Barilko, Johnny McCormack and Cal Gardner had fortified Toronto with a 4–0 lead as the clock ticked away toward the middle of the third period. The cause of the Red Wings appeared hopeless as Toronto captain Ted "Teeder" Kennedy methodically lugged the puck out of his territory toward the Detroit goal.

Kennedy was six feet from the left boards as he reached center ice. Behind him in pursuit was defenseman Jack Stewart of the Wings. Sweeping in from the right side was Howe, who attempted to crash Kennedy amidships. Howe's speed was a trifle too slow for him to hit Kennedy with full force and it appeared the best he could do would be to graze the Leaf player and throw him off balance.

But Howe appeared to miss even that opportunity and, as Kennedy stopped short and then pressed forward, he tumbled, face-first, into the thick wooden side boards.

"I don't know how he got it," said a worried-looking and drawn Kennedy in the noisy Leaf dressing room after the game. "I avoided his check along the boards and didn't feel anything hit me, although he may have struck my stick. It could have happened when he crashed into the boards."

Seconds after Howe rammed the boards his face was a bloody pulp and he lay unconscious on the ice. He had suffered a "stiff concussion" of the head, a bruised cheek-bone and a broken nose. As 13,659 fans sat awestruck by the scene, he was carried off the ice on a stretcher and removed to Harper Hospital where doctors described his condition as "serious."

His head injuries were so serious doctors ordered him into the operating room where neurosurgeons probed for additional injuries. Soon, they decided to operate to relieve pressure on his brain. For several hours there was a question whether Howe would survive the ordeal. He did survive the first-night crisis but remained in critical condition.

Still, doubt remained whether he would live. A

call was put through to Saskatoon where Gordie's mother was urged to take the first plane to Detroit so she could be at her son's bedside. Mrs. Howe, accompanied by her daughter, Mrs. Gladys Lyell, arrived in Detroit on Thursday, two days after the accident.

Gordie wasn't told that his mother was coming to Detroit. When she walked into his room, he exclaimed, "Why, Mom, what are you doing here?"

"You seem just like my old Gordie," she replied, and they embraced.

Dr. C. L. Tomsu, the Red Wings' physician, said the visit from Gordie's mother was better medicine for the injured star than anything a doctor could prescribe. "He still has a headache," said Mrs. Howe, "but he's feeling fine. I certainly feel much better at finding him so well."

But the episode was hardly finished. What started out as a typical brushfire feud between the two rivals soon would erupt into one of the biggest conflagrations in the league's history. It was fed by verbal gasoline poured on by antagonists from both sides. The Red Wing camp charged that it was Kennedy who wantonly injured Howe.

"If he [Kennedy] didn't hit Howe with his stick, why did he skate over and apologize?"

charged Detroit coach Tommy Ivan. "I'm not saying it was deliberate, but it was a check made with the butt end of Kennedy's stick."

Visibly shaken by the chain of events, Kennedy offered to take an oath that he did not cause the injury. "I saw Howe lying on the ice with his face covered with blood," said the Leaf captain, "and I couldn't help thinking what a great player he was and how I hoped he wasn't badly hurt. Then Detroit players started saying I did it with my stick. I knew I hadn't and, as I've always regarded Ivan as a sensible level-headed man, I went over to the Detroit bench and told him I was sorry Howe was hurt, but that I wasn't responsible."

The Toronto camp countercharged that Detroit captain Sid Abel tried to chop down Kennedy with his stick after Howe was injured. The chain reaction of events so disturbed Jim Vipond, sports editor of *The Globe and Mail* of Toronto, that he sharply criticized Abel in an editorial: "Sid Abel, a fine performer and a veteran of the game, who should have known better, disregarded the puck when play finally was resumed. Instead, he slashed at Kennedy's ankle and Ted has a nasty welt to show for it."

Leaf defenseman Garth Boesch suggested that Howe was hurt by his own teammate Jack Stewart's stick, an opinion that was shared by other members of the team. Al Nickleson, who covered the game for *The Globe and Mail,* observed: "From the raised press box, directly across the rink from where the incident occurred, it appeared to this observer that Kennedy, in stopping short, had raised his elbow as a protective gesture and that Howe had struck it, before smashing into the boards with his face as he fell. However, Kennedy repeated that, as far as he knew, no part of his person had touched Howe."

Red Burnett, writing in *The Toronto Daily Star,* added: "Referee George Gravel saw the mishap to Howe, didn't call a penalty and that proves, as far as we are concerned, that Kennedy did not hit Howe."

Soon, the war spilled over into the journalistic realm and Detroit writers began to attack Toronto writers, in print, over their handling of "L'Affaire Howe."

Paul Chandler, who covered the Red Wings for *The Detroit News,* needled his Toronto colleagues with a story headlined: TORONTO TOWN HOT, BOTHERED.

Chandler wrote: "*The Toronto Telegram* has made Kennedy a martyr, an innocent man put to torture by a cruel conspiracy between the Detroit sports writers and the Detroit Red Wings. 'Kennedy Cleared' screamed the Telegram on Page

One of its news section the day after Howe was injured.

"Cleared of what? The paper said Kennedy has been accused of chopping down Howe with the butt-end of a stick and that Detroit papers were assassinating Kennedy. The Telegram even posed a picture to show how the accident took place. They posed three individuals, labelled 'Kennedy,' 'Howe,' and 'Stewart' on skates in Maple Leaf Gardens. In two views they showed 'Howe' speeding behind 'Kennedy' and smashing into the boards."

It didn't take long for the antagonists to find a common enemy and that was NHL President Clarence Campbell who was singled out for his failure to prevent the brutality and violence that both preceded and followed Howe's injury. Bob Murphy in *The Detroit News* said: "Campbell might do anything at any time, but nothing ever showing any real leadership or courage."

Despite the wave of criticism, Campbell quickly took a stand on the Howe case and promptly exonerated Kennedy. He made it clear that game officials had absolved Kennedy of any blame in connection with Howe's injury and he branded "very vicious" Tommy Ivan's charge that Kennedy had "butt-ended" Howe on the play. Campbell pointed out that Kennedy could not have fouled Howe by way of a butt-end.

"Kennedy," said Campbell, "as a right-handed player, had the butt part of his stick tight to the fence as he was going up the ice. He was being checked from his right. The injuries to Howe were on the right side of the head. Kennedy had stopped to avoid the check and Howe went in front of him."

Interpreters of the president's analysis concluded that Howe's right side was furthest away from Kennedy. The Toronto player was further exonerated when Referee George Gravel submitted his report which coincided with the report of linesman Sammy Babcock. It read:

"Jack Stewart carried the puck into the Toronto end and was checked by Kennedy, who carried the puck into the centre zone right close to the fence on the players' bench side. I turned to follow the play and Stewart was trying to check Kennedy and was right close to him. Just as Kennedy crossed the Toronto blue line, I saw Howe cut across toward Kennedy, skating very fast. Just before Howe got to Kennedy, Kennedy passed backhanded and stopped suddenly. Howe just brushed him slightly and crashed headlong into the fence and fell to the ice. Stewart fell on top of him. Play carried on for a few seconds as Toronto had possession."

Campbell said the only official statement he had received from the Detroit club on the Howe injury was that it was "a very unfortunate incident." The president added: "There is no doubt Gravel saw it all from beginning to end. One linesman, Babcock, also had a very good view. Both their reports are substantially the same."

This contrasted sharply with the report in one Detroit paper which quoted Gravel as saying he didn't see the Howe incident and charged incompetence on the part of officials and the league governors. One of those governors was the vitriolic Conn Smythe, manager of the Maple Leafs.

"It seems," Smythe shot back, "every time the Leafs go out to defend the championship they have to defend their right to play. Loose accusations against players have no place in the game. Neither has rough hockey. Kennedy always has been a great and clean player . . . this is the roughest, toughest, hardest and fastest-thinking game in the world today."

Not to be outdone, Mayor Hiram McCallum of Toronto squeezed himself into the controversy and dispatched a message to Kennedy: "The people of Toronto know absolutely no blame in any way can be attached to you for the accident to

Gordie Howe. They are 100 per cent behind you all the way and know you will go on and continue to play wonderful hockey . . . leading the team to the Cup. We regret very much the injury to Howe as he is a great player, but at the same time know that he was the aggressor in attempting to crash you on the boards."

By the time the opening face-off approached for the second game of the semi-finals on Thursday, March 30, a pitch of bitterness had been reached that was of infinite intensity. In the Red Wing dressing room, players were chanting, "Win this one for Gordie." In the Maple Leaf dressing room, there was a grim feeling that the Detroiters were going to try to "get" Kennedy.

They were right, but it is doubtful that even the Toronto players had any idea of the brutality they would encounter.

The game began calmly enough with only two penalties called in the first period as Detroit ran up a two-goal lead on scores by Red Kelly and Sid Abel. Joe Carveth got another goal for the Wings midway in the second period and, for a few more moments, it appeared that rationality would prevail. Then, it happened.

"Somebody pulled an invisible trigger," said Jim Vipond, sports editor of *The Globe and Mail,* "and mayhem broke loose."

It started when Lee Fogolin sent Kennedy rolling to the ice with a stick trip. As play halted and referee Butch Keeling thumbed Fogolin to the penalty box, Ted Lindsay rushed up and cross-checked Kennedy to the ice. Gus Mortson flew at Lindsay and fights broke out all over the ice. About 20 feet out from the Detroit goal, Jim Thomson fell to the ice and Leo Reise bludgeoned him across the head and shoulders with his stick. The Toronto defenseman was defenseless and dazed as Reise, apparently not satisfied, slashed away. Blood flowed. By this time, Kennedy was on the other side of the rink and Reise moved over to put in some stickwork, this time across Kennedy's shoulders.

Lindsay returned and rushed at Kennedy, his stick held high; then Abel rushed, flailing with his fists. A fan grabbed Kennedy and manacled him as other Wings struck the Leaf captain. Toronto goalie Turk Broda, handicapped by 35 pounds of leg pads, trundled to the scene to assist his teammate but Abel and Lindsay persisted in their attempts to get at Kennedy.

Veteran onlookers were stunned by the panoply of terror. "This writer," said Vipond, "has often avowed that no player would intentionally injure another, but not after tonight. There could be nothing more brutal and deliberate than the Detroit players' attempt to even a trumped-up injustice to one of their mates."

The fighting finally subsided only to erupt again in the final minutes of the third period when several other battles kept the referee on a belt line to the penalty box. When the ice had cleared the Wings had won the game and trooped happily into their dressing room with Lindsay at the head of the march yelling, "We won it for Gordie."

Howe, meanwhile, was still in critical condition in Harper Hospital. Doctors had refused to permit him to hear the game or be told the result until the following day.

Kennedy emerged from the fracas with more dignity than most. He never backed away from any of his assailants and left the ice with a discolored eye and a cut above his lip. "He was supposed to be slowed up because of a charley horse," said his boss, Conn Smythe. "He played a terrific game. His line scored our only goal and had no goals scored against it. He's still the greatest hockey player in the world."

Across the hall, Detroit's manager Jack Adams was saying: "The Red Wings are champions of the world . . . and don't forget we played without, possibly, the greatest player in the world—Gordie Howe."

All Kennedy would say was, "The game's over. They won it."

By now, the Howe episode was threatening to move to the courts. The Wings charged that Conn Smythe commented after the injury: "Two years ago Detroit broke my Gus Mortson's leg and last year they broke the jaw of Elmer Lach of Canadiens in the playoffs."

Adams countered: "We are now suing a Montreal newspaperman for $75,000 for saying we broke Lach's jaw. Smythe is taking a lot on himself making the ruling that is to be decided by the Canadian courts."

Antagonists were in agreement on one point, NHL president Campbell was the man who could calm the hairy tempers. "Too much blood and thunder can ruin the game," wrote Tommy Devine in *The Detroit Free Press*. "Campbell would do well to make his warnings against violence sharp and then make them stick."

This time Campbell responded with a loud gavel. He sharpened the teeth of the NHL rules and warned that "very substantial fines and suspensions" would be applied, if necessary, to stop bitter feuding between the Maple Leafs and Red Wings. He ordered the stand-by referee to act as a linesman in future games and ordered the managers and coaches of both teams to a meeting to settle "any possible misunderstandings . . . of what is being done."

"Hockey is a tough and rugged game at the best of times," said Campbell, "but the stick-swinging which took place has no place in the game at any time."

Campbell's statement obliquely indicted the Red Wings and many critics insisted he was speaking directly about Leo Reise's clubbing Jim Thomson over the head, not to mention the attacks on Kennedy. Still, the Red Wings insisted they were innocent.

"Never at any time did I tell any of my players to go out and do anything to that boy [Kennedy]," said Detroit coach Tommy Ivan. "I can only repeat that I did not have any thought of my players seeking revenge. You can confirm that statement by talking to my players. Responsible lads like Red Kelly will back me up. We're not interested in trying to get anybody. We've got to win hockey games and I really want to win this series, but we certainly won't win by doing anything so foolish as to injure players."

Armed with Campbell's edict, referee Bill Chadwick ruled the third game, played at Maple Leaf Gardens in Toronto, with an iron hand. He whistled off Howie Meeker in the opening minute of the game and penalized only two other players. He didn't have to do any more. The players had restored their mental equilibrium and were playing hockey according to the book. The Leafs scored twice in the second period on goals by Joe Klukay and Max Bentley and won the game, 2–0, to take a 2–1 lead in the series.

Detroit tied the series with a 2–1 victory in the fourth game; then the Leafs went ahead again, blanking the Wings, 2–0, to skate to within a game of winning the Cup for the fourth straight year. But Detroit still had some energy left even though it now was apparent that their star, Howe, would be lost to them for the playoffs. They defeated Toronto, 4–0, in the sixth game, carrying the semi-final to a seventh and deciding game at Detroit.

The final game of the 1950 series is regarded as one of hockey's classics. The teams battled through three periods of regulation time without a goal being scored. Checking remained close through the opening eight minutes of the sudden death overtime. Olympia, that night, was not an arena for the weak-hearted.

Coach Tommy Ivan sent out a line of George Gee, Steve Black and Joe Carveth against Toron-

Gordie Howe lifts his stick high in the air as he skates around fallen Montreal Canadiens goalie Charlie Hodge after breaking Maurice Richard's scoring record with the 545th goal of his career, November 10, 1963. Billy McNeill (19) assisted Howe on the goal. WIDE WORLD PHOTOS

Here he is on November 11, 1963, in a game against the Boston Bruins. Boston goalie Ed Johnson and defenseman Leo Boivin aren't cooperating. WIDE WORLD PHOTOS

Gordie Howe (9), Norm Ullman (7), and Ted Lindsay (center) launch a concentrated attack on New York Rangers goalie Marcel Paille during a 1964-season game at Madison Square Garden. Paille seems to have the situation well in hand, however. Helping out is Ranger Jim Neilson (5). WIDE WORLD PHOTOS

Gordie Howe rides Jim Roberts, of the Montreal Canadiens, and the puck to the ice in front of the Detroit goal during the first period of a Stanley Cup game in 1966. Detroit goalie Hank Bassen, substituting for the injured Roger Crozier can't quite believe it. WIDE WORLD PHOTOS

Gordie Howe scores his 714th career goal in regular season play during the first period of the Detroit-Chicago game at Olympia Stadium, while Detroit's Frank Mahovlich (27) and Hawk goalie Dave Dryden (9) watch. Howe scored as Detroit defeated Chicago, 5 to 1, in February, 1969.

to's Max Bentley, Fleming Mackell and Vic Lynn. The Leafs had Bill Juzda and Bill Barilko on defense, while Detroit's defenders were Jack Stewart and Leo Reise.

Gee, Black and Carveth launched a dangerous rush for the Wings, backed by Stewart and Reise. Several times the puck bounced dangerously close to the goal line, only to be cleared; but the Leafs couldn't quite get the disk out of their own zone. Finally, Gee captured the puck and slid it across the ice to Reise, who was standing near the blue line 60 feet from the goal.

His shot went straight to the net where goalie Turk Broda appeared to have the short side blocked with his skate, pad and stick. But the puck bounced over Broda's stick and hit the back of the net. Detroit had won, 1–0.

The final round against the New York Rangers might have been anti-climactic except that it, too, was decided in sudden death overtime in the seventh game. In fact, the Wings and Rangers went into the second overtime before Detroit's Pete Babando took a pass from George Gee and backhanded a 15-foot shot past goalie Chuck Rayner to give the Wings a 4–3 victory and the Stanley Cup.

Howe was in the arena, and when the ancient

silver mug was pushed out to center ice, the 13,095 fans spontaneously chanted: "We want Howe! We want Howe!" As Gordie gingerly stepped on the ice, Lindsay grabbed his hat and sent it flying into the stands, then fondly tapped the head of his star linemate and joked, "You big lucky stiff. You sit in the seats and watch us go out and make a couple of thousand dollars for you."

And when the ceremony at mid-ice had ended, Howe was given the Cup and carried it through the milling, cheering crowd to the Detroit dressing room. He was well on his road to recovery, ready for even greater accomplishments than before.

Chapter Six

LESS THAN three months after his near-fatal injury, Howe was well enough to start playing baseball in the Northern Saskatchewan League. By the time he reported to the Red Wings' training camp he was in near-perfect condition, and, as the 1950–51 season opened, Howe pronounced himself ready to go.

Still, his teammates and opponents wondered if he would play as aggressively as he had before the accident. Had he left a little bit of heart back in that hospital room? Would he be gun-shy? Would he occasionally take his eye off the puck and glance about for a defender when he was near the boards? Would he slow himself down just a bit at the blue line and perhaps lose that valuable half-step? Would he pass up the opportunity to throw a hard check at an enemy forward?

Howe answered those doubts—and perhaps his

own subconscious fears as well—in the best of all possible ways. He went out and scored 43 goals and added 43 assists—good enough to lead the league in both goals and total points.

The Wings again finished first, only to be upset by Montreal in the first round of the Stanley Cup playoffs. The loss of the Cup, by the way, was no fault of Howe's. He had four goals and three assists in the six-game series.

During the 1950–51 campaign, Howe also reached a personal milestone—the first of many. He scored his 100th NHL goal on the night of February 17, 1951. The goalie was Montreal's Gerry McNeil. The game was played at the Montreal Forum, and Howe's goal proved to be the winning score. But most embarrassing of all, it came on "Rocket Richard Night."

Then again, perhaps that 100th goal was but an omen of things to come. For at the end of the season Howe displaced Richard at right wing on the first team of All-Stars. More than that, Howe was fast displacing Richard as the most celebrated player in professional hockey. As we noted before, the 1940s were Richard's era and the 1950s belonged to Howe. The question still being debated by hockey fans and experts is, taking into account the entire careers of both, which of the two was the greater?

To begin with, Richard's style of play—explosive, aggressive and at all times colorful—reminds one of Babe Ruth. Howe, on the other hand, can probably best be likened to Joe DiMaggio, although he has displayed Ruthian qualities on many occasions. Richard was first and foremost a scorer. Probably no player in the history of professional hockey was as fearsome as Richard inside the enemy's blue line.

In Montreal, for example, they still talk about what is referred to simply as "the Boston goal." Richard scored it late in the third period of a Stanley Cup playoff game against Boston in 1952. The Bruins had just completed a rush on the Canadien goal. Richard retrieved the disk in front of the Montreal net and started up ice. He swerved around a Boston wingman who was trying to check him, cut to the right boards at the red line and headed toward Bruin ice.

At the Boston line Richard fended off a Bruin defenseman with his left arm, but still was steered into the corner to the right of the Boston net. It appeared that the puck would be frozen there. But somehow, Richard managed to break free from the defenseman. With a swoop of his stick he recovered the puck and skated laterally toward the Boston goal. With a quick feint, Richard brought the goal tender to his knees. Then he fired into the upper right-hand corner of the net. Richard's score broke a 1–1 tie and gave Montreal the game.

In scoring territory then, Richard was a furious and feverish hockey player, completely obsessed with scoring. "When he came flying in toward you with the puck on his stick," says Chicago goalie Glenn Hall, "Richard's eyes were all lit up, flashing and gleaming like a pinball machine."

Richard, however, had relatively little use for the other aspects of the game. His defensive play was often loose, sometimes downright sloppy. He never was much of a checker. Nor was he overly concerned with the assist column of the scoring sheet. Given the option of shooting or passing to a teammate with better position, Richard would shoot. This may seem like nit-picking, since Richard still ranks as the most explosive scorer in the annals of the NHL, but it does help to point up the major difference between the Rocket and Gordie Howe.

Several years ago, the six coaches then in the National Hockey League were asked to define the best qualities of both Howe and Richard. They replied that Richard had the most accurate shot in the league, and also was the game's best man on a breakaway. Howe, they said, was the best puck-carrier, best play-maker, top passer, and the league's smartest player.

More recently, "Boom-Boom" Geoffrion was asked whether in his opinion Howe or Richard was the greater hockey player. Geoffrion responded by saying: "From the waist down, I'll take the Rocket. From the waist up, give me Howe. Howe could kill penalties, pass, and do almost everything. The Rocket concentrated on scoring. But from the blue line to the other team's post, give me the Rocket. If my team needed a goal, I would want the Rocket with the puck near the boards."

Howe was—and still is—the complete hockey player. Richard was not. Howe is an outstanding checker and defensive player. He works equally as well as a penalty killer and as the key man in the Detroit power play. In other words, he excels in all phases of the game.

Certainly, Howe loves to score. But he also derives great satisfaction from setting up a teammate for a goal. In the last game of the 1959–60 season, for example, Detroit rookie Murray Oliver (now with the Maple Leafs) needed one goal to collect a cash bonus for netting 20 goals in his maiden season. Midway through the game Howe told Oliver: "The next time we're on ice, get in front of the net." Oliver followed instructions. Howe carried to the blue line, shot, and Oliver tipped the puck in for the score. Then, in an uncharacteristic burst of bravado, Howe skated to the Detroit bench and called out: "Anyone else need any bonus money?"

A few seasons later, Howe was working under a bonus set-up that paid him $1,000 for his first 35 goals, and $100 for each goal thereafter.

In a game against Boston, Howe was credited with the first goal of the night. He skated over to the official scorer and asked for a correction, explaining that Parker MacDonald was entitled to the goal. In the second period the Wings scored again. Again Howe received credit for the goal. Again he disagreed with the official scorer and the goal was credited to Alex Delvecchio.

But getting back to the Howe-Richard comparison. Perhaps the best capsule comment on the question of which one ranks at the top came from a Montreal cab driver who was quoted in a *New Yorker* article by Herbert Warren Wind. Said the Montreal cabbie:

"Gordie Howe is the best hockey player I have ever seen. Maurice Richard? Marvelous hockey player. But I think Gordie Howe is stronger than Maurice Richard. You know, he is more the artist.

He does not force. He takes it easy. He is all the time like me smoking a cigarette in my taxi."

Howe's rise to the "superstar" class coincided with the start of a four-year period during which the Red Wings overshadowed the Canadiens, who, until then, had been regarded as the premier players of professional hockey. Beginning with the 1951–52 campaign and continuing through the 1954–55 season, Detroit finished atop the league, while Montreal placed second. During that same period, the Wings won three Stanley Cup championships, and the Canadiens took the Cup but once.

Howe regards the 1951–52 team as the best Detroit club he has played on. And with good reason. That season Detroit compiled 100 points in 70 games—while second-place Montreal picked up 78 points. In the first round of the Stanley Cup playoffs, the Wings beat Toronto four straight. In the final round against the Canadiens, the Wings again won four straight.

"The way we were playing," Howe says in talking about the Stanley Cup sweep, "I think we could have won 35 straight."

Certainly, Howe appeared so omnipotent on the ice one suspected he could score at his pleasure. I recall seeing him demoralize the Maple Leafs in the third game of the Stanley Cup semi-final round in Toronto on March 29, 1952, shooting with bomb-sight accuracy and brushing past enemy tanks as if they were made of cardboard.

When Gordie was at the top of his game, as he was that night, he skittered effortlessly from one end of the rink to another, like a water bug on a pond. His shot had a deceptive quality about it. Instead of being heralded first with a flamboyant wind-up—as is Bobby Hull's slap shot of today—Howe's blast was unobtrusive, like a gun shot felling a beast without any warning because of a silencer over its muzzle. So it was with Howe's release—quiet, true, but packing enormous velocity until it hit the twine behind the net.

Unlike Rocket Richard, Howe occasionally would return to his boyhood traits and just plain fool around with his ability—and his opponents. In that memorable Toronto game—which, incidentally, Detroit won 6–2—I recall Howe breaking away from the entire Leaf team at center ice and cruising in on rotund Turk Broda, helplessly alone in front of the Leaf net.

Almost dreamily, Gordie loped along the left side, nonchalantly executed a couple of feints that lured Broda several feet out of the net and flopping on to the ice, and then, with nothing but the six feet of yawning cage in front of him, Howe playfully shot for the far right post, trying for a billiard carom shot. This was the only challenge left for him. The puck nicked the right post and slipped harmlessly into the corner.

Howe worry? Why should he? Next time he wouldn't fool around, and the puck would go in.

That year, Howe scored 47 goals in regular season play and added 39 assists to lead the league in total points and goals. He also was awarded the first of his six Hart trophies as the league's Most Valuable Player.

Chapter Seven

THE YEAR 1951 also marked another turning point in Gordie Howe's life. He met his future wife, Colleen Joffa. "I didn't know anything about hockey then," she recalls, "and I'd never heard of Gordie Howe.

"The first time I heard the name I was a senior in high school and it was the morning after he had been hurt in the Stanley Cup game against Toronto. When I came down to breakfast, my dad was storming around the kitchen. He was a Red Wings' fan and he was mad."

She met Gordie a year later at a bowling alley located three blocks from Detroit's Olympia. The owner, Joe Evans, introduced them. A few minutes later he asked her: "How did you like meeting a celebrity?"

"Is that a celebrity?" she said.

"Are you kidding?" Evans countered. "That's Gordie Howe of the Red Wings."

They were married April 15, 1953, in Detroit's Calvary Presbyterian Church. Ted Lindsay, Reggie Sinclair and Marty Pavelich of the Red Wings were ushers. Lindsay's wife, Pat, was the matron of honor.

The Howes have four children—three boys and a girl. The eldest, Martin, is named after Pavelich. The second boy is named Mark. Then there's Cathy. And the youngest, Murray, is named after Murray Oliver. Both Marty and Mark play hockey. Of the two, Gordie has said that Mark has the best chance of making it to the "pros," but, of course, it is too soon to tell.

Significantly, it is Mark who has worn number nine on his uniform. "That represented a big decision," Howe admits. "Marty is a thin-skinned guy, whereas you can't hurt Mark's feelings. So I figured he'd be better equipped to handle the abuse and attention that goes with carrying my number. Boy, he takes it too!"

Mark, who has been skating since the age of five, also has a great confidence in his natural ability to play hockey. He once confided to his famous father that he had learned the secret of scoring on rebound shots. "You have!" Howe declared. "Well, you better let me in on it."

Gordie emphasizes one thing, however. "I'll never force either of them into hockey. I want them to get the education I missed. If they can combine hockey and schooling, so much the better."

Gordie's wife attends every Detroit home game. Once, when she was asked if she worries about her husband being injured, she gave this thoughtful reply:

"Sometimes—especially when he's already playing with an injury, and when I can see somebody on the other team getting mad and banging around. I hope they get him off the ice before he does hit Gordie.

"But what you think about more," she continued, "is whether he's getting his goals and assists, and whether the team is winning. If he goes five or six games without a goal, it begins to bother him. He doesn't say anything, but he gets very quiet."

Defenseman Marcel Pronovost bears out Mrs. Howe's statement.

"If Gordie worries about a slump, he keeps it deep inside him," Pronovost says. "He never shows it. It was a treat to be on a team with him."

When the Red Wings are playing at home, a typical game day for Gordie Howe goes something like this:

He usually wakes up about 10 o'clock and breakfasts on two eggs (scrambled) and cereal. After breakfast he dresses, then drives to the Olympia for the team's noon meeting. The meetings are generally short.

Howe is back home by one o'clock. He may putter around his garage for a few minutes, or he might watch television—anything to kill the time and ease the tension before the puck is dropped at center ice for the start of another game.

He eats a combination lunch and dinner at two o'clock. Howe prefers ground round steak to regular steak. "The round steak is more tender," he explains. "I haven't had a regular steak at home for years." At three o'clock he goes upstairs for a two-hour nap. By 5:30 he is showered, shaved, dressed, and ready to drive to the Olympia. En route to a game, Howe invariably wears a white shirt, tie and suit. He arrives at the Olympia shortly before six o'clock and goes directly to the Detroit dressing room.

Once there, he carefully removes his dental bridge, wraps it in a handkerchief and places it in a pocket of his jacket. Then, dressing quickly, he pulls on his long woolen underwear, his white woolen socks and the long red-and-white stockings. Then he puts on his shin guards, his jersey and his pants. Finally, his skates go on—first the right one, then the left. After that, Howe goes to the stick rack and selects one from the half-dozen or so that have his name and number printed on them. They are specially made to his specifications.

If there is time before the warm-up, Howe will play gin rummy with a teammate, or tackle a crossword puzzle. Working the puzzles is one of his favorite pastimes.

He is a puzzle addict and has been one since his earliest days in hockey. Friends say he likes the puzzles because they help increase his vocabulary and compensate for his lack of schooling. Howe likes to tell of the policeman at the Olympia "who thinks I'm the world champion with the puzzles." It happened this way, according to Gordie:

"One of our guys had taken a Toronto paper back to Detroit. There was a tough crossword puzzle in it. By accident I noticed the same puzzle had run in the Detroit paper one day earlier. So I memorized the key words. At practice, somebody mentioned this puzzle from Toronto. I asked for the paper. And while I was sitting on the bench waiting for my turn on ice, I filled in all the blanks in a couple of minutes. One of the policemen was watching. And when I got through, he thought I was one of the original Quiz Kids."

Another of Howe's favorite pastimes is instructing youngsters in the art of hockey. When Gordie is home, he can usually count on two or three visits a day from neighborhood kids, some of whom drop by to ask him a few questions. Others just stand and stare at him for a few minutes, too awed by Howe's presence to talk, and too dazzled by him to leave.

Once a week or so, Howe will spirit a group of neighborhood youngsters into the Olympia for a "sneak" practice session. Then, in mid-August, at a time when most players are wrapping up their vacations and preparing for training camp, Howe is the feature attraction at a hockey school conducted at the Olympia. He also operates his own hockey school in suburban St. Clair Shores.

"I enjoy teaching kids," Howe explains. "I think coaching would be fun . . . a lot of headaches, of course, but I'd like to do it."

There are some who believe that Gordie Howe is too nice a guy to coach. But Sid Abel named Howe an assistant coach in 1961 and consults Gordie on player moves, team problems and game strategy. In 1967 he actually let Gordie handle the team for one game.

Howe shrugs off the comment that he might not have a tough enough personality for coaching. "I'd like to do it when I finish playing," he says, "simply because this game has given me everything. Look at me. A kid from the West. I met and married a beautiful girl, and have a nice home and family and I've met so many nice people. I've been accepted and it's all due to hockey."

The selection of Howe as an assistant coach was a popular choice with his teammates. Marcel Pronovost, who was Howe's roommate at the time, described "Number 9" this way:

"Gordie Howe is a remarkable fellow on and off the ice. Everybody knows what he can do on a hockey rink. It's what he does off the ice, at home and on trips, that amazes me.

"He's never too busy to give autographs. On the road he often spends two or three hours answering mail that has accumulated at Detroit Olympia, sending out autographed pictures. It must cost him $300 to $400 a season in stamps alone.

"He's a great influence on the younger players, too," Pronovost continued. "Even though he was listed as an assistant coach he never tried to exert authority of any kind. If a young fellow asked him for advice or instruction, though, he responded immediately."

As for Howe himself, he has his own ideas about what makes a good coach. Writing in his column for the *Toronto Daily Star* syndicate, Howe noted:

"In my book there are two kinds of coaches —the fellow who likes to criticize and the fellow who likes to teach. Let's face it, coaches get a little frustrated at times. Sitting on the bench, they can't do a thing about what's going on out on the ice during a game.

"You have the old 'hard hats' who believe in nothing but work, work, work, and that eventually the problems will solve themselves. And you have the coaches who criticize—who say 'no, no, no, you did it all wrong. Go back and try again.' Actually, they are not teaching."

Howe has no use for the "hard hat" or the constant critic.

"Sure," he says, "sometimes there are bad habits you've had that you'll lapse back into. And that's when a fellow like Sid Abel, who was a great hockey player himself, will note these things. He's not just a gate opener. He'll come in after a period and say, 'You're doing this wrong,' or 'You are doing this too often,' and tell you what you should do. That's what I call a teaching coach."

Then Howe adds this final word about coaching techniques:

"You appreciate it when you're treated like a gentleman. You're happy. And I think the fellow who is happy can produce much better."

One of Howe's closest friends in hockey is Murray Oliver. Oliver, who has known Howe since his own rookie days, takes issue with those who contend that Gordie is a dirty player. "He's tough all right," Oliver remarks, "but he has to be. Hockey's a tough game."

Oliver first saw Howe when he went to the Detroit training camp while still a member of a Red Wing farm club.

"When the Wings were on ice I sat there with my mouth open," Oliver recalls. "I just watched and admired Gordie. I couldn't get over the way he moved so effortlessly and the fact that he worked as hard or harder than anyone else, even though he was a 'superstar.'

"I'll never forget the day I got the word that the Wings had called me up from Edmonton," Oliver continued. "It was my 22nd birthday and I flew into Chicago to join the team. Later that night I met Gordie for the first time as we dressed for the game against the Black Hawks. All he said was 'welcome.' "

Oliver sat out the first three games. But the Wings were in a slump and, finally, Sid Abel decided to shake up the Detroit offense. He put Oliver on a line with Howe and another youngster, Gary Aldcorn.

"Our line played well in the first period," Oliver relates, "but it wasn't until the second period that I scored my first NHL goal. Gordie passed to Aldcorn, who relayed the puck to me. I shot quickly and beat Harry Lumley in the Boston nets. That gave me the confidence I needed. I felt as though I belonged.

"That same night we had a few hours to kill before we were to take a plane to New York. Gordie came over and invited me to sit with him in the lobby of the airport.

"He told me that he and Aldcorn had asked the coach to give me a chance to center their line. We talked for quite awhile, not so much about hockey but about baseball. I once wanted to be a big league ballplayer and even had a tryout with the Cleveland Indians. Gordie seemed impressed. He's very much interested in the game.

"It got to be a growing friendship. We spent a lot of time together. He invited me to his house for Christmas dinner and I met his wife and children. Mark took a particular liking to me. And when his mother took him to the games, Mark rooted for me to score goals rather than his daddy."

Oliver and Aldcorn were traded to the Bruins on January 24th, 1961, for Leo Labine and Vic Stasiuk.

"After the deal was made," Oliver remembers, "Gordie took me aside and said, 'I didn't think they'd let you go. I knew about it, but didn't have the heart to tell you.'

"That night Gordie asked that I go to his house

for dinner. He and Colleen were very sympathetic. I spent the night there. In the morning I felt much better."

The Bruins played the Wings a week later and Oliver faced Howe as an opponent for the first time.

"Early in the game," Oliver recalls, "Gordie was on the ice during a power play and I was killing a Boston penalty. I had control of the puck and slid it past him. Then I tried to get around him to pick it up again. He nonchalantly held out his forearm as I went by and stopped me cold.

"Seconds later, before a face-off, Gordie skated over to me and asked, 'I didn't hit you in the face, did I?' Here I was on another team and he was still concerned about me. It wasn't easy to get accustomed to playing without him.

"I'm in a better position now that I'm on another team to appreciate Gordie's tremendous talent. I can really watch him from the other side of the ice."

One of Oliver's Boston teammates is less attached to the Red Wings' star. "When we saw Gordie wasn't out in the warmups," he said, recalling one of the games Howe missed some seasons back, "we went to the dressing room and had a party."

Howe, his wife and their children live in a

$60,000 home in Lathrup Village, a suburban community located some ten miles from the center of Detroit.

Detroit itself is a major sports city in every sense of the word. In addition to the Wings, Detroit houses the baseball Tigers, the football Lions and the pro basketball Pistons. Yet for the last 15 years or so, Gordie Howe has been Detroit's number one sports hero.

Howe is to the Motor City what Ted Williams was to Boston, or what Warren Spahn was to Milwaukee; what Bart Starr is to Green Bay, Mickey Mantle is to New York, or Wilt Chamberlain is to Philadelphia.

In the course of a year, Howe receives hundreds of invitations to address social, civic, charitable and athletic organizations. He accepts as many of the invitations as his schedule permits. At any important function in Detroit, Howe's name is invariably on the guest list as a representative of the athletic fraternity. He also lends his name to a number of civic functions. Not too long ago, for instance, he helped raise funds for the Detroit Symphony Orchestra.

Howe's popularity extends far beyond Detroit, however. A few years ago a Canadian television station conducted a poll, flashing the pictures and names of a dozen famous Canadians on the screen.

Researchers later asked 1,000 selected viewers to identify each of the 12 by occupation. Howe placed second in the poll as 88 per cent of those asked correctly identified him as a hockey player. The top man in the poll was Prime Minister Lester Pearson.

Howe admits quite frankly that he enjoys his fame and the privileges that go with it. When he drives across the border into Canada, for example, he is waved through without question. If a customs officer does stop Howe it's to ask how he's feeling and how many goals he expects to score.

Howe's annual salary of more than $40,000 for playing hockey is only part of his income. In conjunction with his hockey school in St. Clair, Howe is part owner of Gordie Howe's Hockeyland. He also has a contract with Eaton's—a chain of Canadian department stores for which he does public relations and tests sports equipment. He writes a hockey column three times a week for the *Toronto Daily Star* Syndicate and the column now runs in approximately 70 papers. And back in 1963, Campbell's Soup Company brought out a hard-cover book entitled, *Hockey—Here's Howe.* Gordie put the book together with the aid of a Toronto broadcaster and hockey writer, Bob Hesketh.

Among his business contacts, Howe is regarded

as a shrewd negotiator. But when asked if he is as good a businessman as he is a hockey player, Howe laughs and replies: "Heck, no!"

Then he tells about an earlier business experience with Al Kaline, the All-Star outfielder for the Detroit Tigers.

"We were manufacturers' representatives," Howe relates. "Everybody said we were successful. Heck, we represented four concerns and three went under."

Gordie also runs a wholesale hockey and ski supply company. He became interested in skiing through his wife. "She really likes the sport," Howe says. "Me? Well, the two of us went skiing at Aspen [Colorado] and I skied for three miles. I mean I skied for one and fell two."

Howe's willingness to poke fun at himself despite his exalted position is just one of the reasons he is so popular with his teammates and the hockey public. Naturally, Howe participates in all the team's bantering. But his joking remarks are almost always directed at himself, not against someone else. After 21 years in the NHL, there isn't a question that hasn't been asked at least a half-dozen times. Yet, he rarely brushes off a reporter. And no matter how silly or irrelevant a question might be, Howe invariably answers it fully and seriously.

He receives roughly three times as much mail as the rest of the Detroit team combined, and he tries to answer all letters himself. And for all of his fame—all of his years in the limelight—Howe is still somewhat shy. At public appearances, or while being interviewed on television, he has a nervous blink. In private, the blink is less noticeable, but still there. "Last season," he chuckles, "the management sent Paul Henderson to Arizona to cure his breathing problem. The year before they sent Roger Crozier to Florida for a mid-season rest. But I've been blinking for 20 years and never got out of Detroit."

"Gordie," says Sid Abel, "is the same nice guy he was when I first played with him. Except that he's older and more mature."

Chapter Eight

THE 1951–52 season marked the end of the Production Line. Sid Abel was traded to the Chicago Black Hawks at his own request. The Hawks had offered him the dual job of player-coach. So, at the start of the 1952–53 campaign, Howe and Lindsay had a new center—the affable, easy-going, but talented Alex Delvecchio. It would be inaccurate to say that Abel was not missed. Players of his caliber are few and far between. But it also would be inaccurate to say that Delvecchio was not an adequate replacement. He was all of that—and then some.

Centering for Howe and Lindsay, Delvecchio scored 16 goals and added 43 assists. He was named to the second team of All-Stars. Howe and Lindsay, of course, were named to the first team.

For Howe, in fact, the 1952–53 campaign was the best of all his many great seasons.

He led the league in scoring with 95 points and in goals scored with 49. His 49 goals were just one short of the single-season record then held by Rocket Richard. Both Hull and Geoffrion later tied Richard's mark. Hull, of course, shattered the record with his 54 goals during the 1965–66 season and again with 52 goals in the 1966–67 season. Howe's 1952–53 performance also earned him his second consecutive Hart Trophy. He thereby matched a feat of two hockey immortals of the 1930's—Boston's Eddie Shore and Montreal's Howie Morenz. Oh, yes. Howe played 15 games of the 1952–53 season with a broken right wrist. He broke the wrist in a Christmas night game, had the wrist placed in a cast, and played out the full 70-game schedule as if in A-1 condition.

Entering the Stanley Cup playoffs, the Wings were a prohibitive choice to repeat as champions. But the Boston Bruins, who had finished third in regular season play, pulled one of the major upsets of the Cup competition and ousted the Wings in six games. Howe did his best to avert the upset, scoring two goals and adding five assists.

Gordie repeated as scoring leader the following season, this time with 33 goals and 48 assists for a total of 81 points. Again he was named to the first team of All-Stars. But he missed out on the Hart Trophy. That award went to goalie Al Rollins of the Chicago Black Hawks, who had finished in last place with a total of 12 wins in 70 games played.

The Wings did regain the Stanley Cup, however, as Howe scored four goals and added five assists in the playoff competition. He also chalked up 31 minutes in penalties.

As a team, the Wings maintained their championship touch during the 1954–55 campaign. Again they finished atop the league, and did so even though Howe had what was for him a sub-par season. Missing six games because of a leg injury, Howe managed but 29 goals and 33 assists for a total of 62 points. As a result, he failed for the first time in six years to make either the first or second team of All-Stars.

But being Gordie Howe, the type of player who always manages to rise to the occasion, he proceeded to lead the Wings to their second consecutive Stanley Cup by notching nine goals and adding 11 assists in 11 playoff games. That still ranks as one of the top performances by an individual player in the history of the Cup competition.

The following season Detroit failed to finish in first place for the first time in eight years. The Wings were second, behind Montreal. Howe had 38 goals and 41 assists for a total of 79 points. And he was selected for the second team of All-Stars behind Richard, who enjoyed his last truly great season. Montreal went on to defeat the Wings in the finals of Stanley Cup play. In 10 playoff games, Howe had only three goals, but did chip in with nine assists.

Detroit bounced back during the 1956–57 campaign, finishing in first place. Howe captured the scoring title with a total of 89 points on 44 goals and 45 assists. Again the Wings went into the Stanley Cup playoffs favored to win. Again the Boston Bruins turned the tables, ousting the Wings in five games during the opening round. And since that time, the Wings have never quite scaled the heights again. Detroit has captured only one league title since, and the Wings have not won another Stanley Cup. During that period of relative drought, what the Wings have accomplished is due in large measure to Gordie Howe.

To most hockey observers, the years between 1952 and 1957 marked the second phase of Gordie Howe's career.

Following Sid Abel's departure from Detroit, Howe and Lindsay formed the most productive and fearsome one-two punch in the history of professional hockey. Yet, they did not take their success for granted. Despite their pre-eminence in the world of hockey, Howe and Lindsay continued their habit of practicing together after the regular practice sessions. They learned each other's moves and perfected their timing to the point where they could hit one another with passes more by instinct than by sight.

On one of their favorite plays Howe would carry across the opposing team's blue line, then would skate down the left side, then cut sharply toward the goalmouth. Without looking, Howe would whip a cross-ice pass to a point just to the left of the net. Lindsay and the puck would arrive at the same time. And more often than not, Ted would snap the disk past the helpless goalie.

During this second phase, however, Howe's critics noted a tendency on his part to let some of the other players on the team perform the rigorous chores of hockey—the forechecking and backchecking. Not that Howe didn't do well in these areas. It's just that he might have done even better if he had applied himself more diligently to the tasks at hand.

But as the fortunes of the Wings began to fall following the 1956–57 season, Howe took on more responsibility. In so doing he reached full maturity as both a hockey player and a person and entered the third and final phase of his fabulous career.

When the Wings were locked in a tight game,

for example, Howe would skate with his own line, then fill in for a full turn on one of the other lines. He became the balance-wheel of the Detroit power play, sometimes working from the point position, at other times muscling his way in front of the enemy cage for a tip-in or rebound shot. When the Wings were a man short, Howe went out as a penalty killer, and his very presence on ice often forced the opposing team to play more conservatively. For even though the other club was playing with five skaters to Detroit's four, the enemy forces still had to guard against the type of miscue that would give Howe a break-away opportunity.

Between 1957 and 1964, Howe averaged between 40 and 45 minutes per game on ice—twice the ice time put in by most NHL forwards. While Howe's playing time has been cut by the advancing years, he still works every minute that he is on the ice.

Howe backchecks . . . forechecks . . . carries the puck from his own zone into enemy territory . . . normally draws coverage of the top scorer on the opposing team . . . sets up plays with astonishing regularity . . . and, of course, scores goals.

"Howe has rewritten the entire game," says one NHL official. That he has, especially in two vital areas.

It was Howe who first used the wrist slap shot

with any degree of regularity. In his book, *Hockey —Here's Howe,* Gordie described the wrist slap shot this way:

"The blade of the stick should come back waist high or higher on the back swing and should hit the puck cleanly off the heel. Tighten your grip too much and your stick will turn and the puck will wind up in the corner. Snap your wrists as you hit the puck. Keep your eye on the puck because you can 'fan' on it all too easily, which can be a little embarrassing."

Howe, needless to say, is seldom embarrassed.

Gordie also changed the basic pattern of attack in professional hockey. Under his leadership, Detroit abandoned the position play used by all other NHL clubs in favor of a wide-open, nonrestrictive type of assault that has the forwards sweep down ice in a series of criss-cross designs. Montreal now favors that type of attack and to a degree the Canadiens are now more adept at it than the Wings. But the strategy was formulated by Howe for the Wings. In his book, Howe explained why he favors the "play-it-by-ear" attack.

"Many times, when I hit the blue line," Howe wrote, "I have no idea what I'm going to do to put the puck in the net. The more expert a player becomes with every shot in the bag, the less time he wastes worrying about it, and the more worrisome he is to the goalkeeper. In a nutshell, there never has been a good goal-scorer in hockey who wasn't good at shooting the puck in many different ways."

Howe then goes on to detail the type of shots he prefers.

"In organized hockey," Howe writes, "a goalie will feel like thanking you if you raise the puck; it's easier for him to stop it with his body and his glove. The shots at his ankles, or just above, are the ones that give him the most trouble. This area is where most goals are scored—on low, hard shots. The next best target is high in the corners, preferably the corner on the side where the hand is holding the stick."

Gordie's influence on his Detroit teammates is evident off-ice as well as on. Soon after being named assistant coach, Howe suggested that a rookie and a veteran be paired as roommates when Detroit is on the road. Perhaps recalling his own painful days as a shy rookie, Howe reasoned that pairing a newcomer with a veteran would make the younger player feel he was part of the team more quickly than if he roomed with another rookie. Howe's suggestion was adopted and that's the way it is on the Detroit club today.

In addition, whenever a new player joins the Wings, be he fresh from the minors or a seasoned player traded to Detroit from one of the other NHL teams, the newcomer is invited to dinner by Howe at the first opportunity.

Just prior to his retirement at the end of the 1965–66 season, defenseman Bill Gadsby, who finished his 20 years in the NHL with the Wings, offered this comment on Detroit's ability to remain in the thick of the league race year-after-year despite a scarcity of top-flight talent:

"On paper, Montreal, Chicago and Toronto look like they have much superior teams. Well, we have a dedicated coach, we play hard hockey, and in Howe we have the most inspirational player in the league. When the young kids on our club see how Gordie hustles at his age, going into the corner after the puck and twisting and spinning and coming out of the damned thing—why, it lifts the team. He's the guy who makes the Wings go."

Or, as Dave Keon, the Toronto Maple Leaf star, once put it, prior to the resurgence of the New York Rangers in 1967:

"There are four strong teams in the league and two weak ones. The weak ones are Boston and New York. The strong ones are Toronto, Chicago, Montreal, and Gordie Howe."

Chapter Nine

THE WINGS tumbled to third place during the 1957–58 season—and that marked the first time in 11 years that they had finished lower than second in the league standings. Howe did his best to check the slide, netting 33 goals and adding 44 assists for a total of 77 points. That total did not lead the league. Montreal's Dickie Moore captured the scoring crown that year with 84 points. But in acknowledgement of his over-all play, and his contributions to a relatively weak Detroit team, Howe was named winner of the Hart Trophy—his fourth MVP award and his second in succession.

In the Stanley Cup playoffs, Montreal ousted the Wings in four games. Howe, with a goal and an assist, experienced his worst Cup series since his second season in the league.

The following year, the fortunes of the Wings plummeted to an all-time low. For the first time in the history of the club, Detroit finished in last place—six points behind the fifth-place Rangers.

Just about every Red Wing but Howe was dragged down with the team. Gordie maintained his superior style of play by scoring 32 goals and adding 46 assists for a total of 78 points. That year, however, he wound up on the second team of All-Stars, finishing behind Andy Bathgate of the Rangers. Bathgate had 88 points and succeeded Howe as winner of the Hart Trophy.

The following season, however, Howe regained the Hart award as the Wings made their way back to fourth place. Gordie had "just" 73 points that year. But again, his leadership and inspirational style of play had lifted Detroit out of mediocrity and into the Stanley Cup playoffs. The Wings were bounced out of the Cup competition in the first round, however, losing to the Maple Leafs in six games.

The Wings were fourth again in 1960–61 and again they met the Leafs in the first round of the Stanley Cup playoffs. This time Detroit came out on top, only to bow to the Black Hawks in the Cup finals.

In gaining the fourth and final playoff spot two years running, the Wings had nosed out the Rangers, who finished fifth both seasons. In the 1961–62 campaign, New York got a measure of revenge—placing fourth, four points ahead of the Wings. The battle for fourth place was decided during a late-season game at Madison Square Garden. The game still rates as one of the most dramatic in National Hockey League history. And, of course, Gordie Howe had a hand in making it so.

But before getting to that game, let's back-track a bit. As we mentioned before, Howe had scored the 100th goal of his career at the Montreal Forum in 1951. Goal Number 200 came February 15, 1953, at Chicago. The goalie was Al Rollins. It was Howe's 422nd NHL game. And the Wings won by a score of 4 to 1. Howe's next scoring milestone—goal Number 300—came at Detroit on the night of February 7, 1956. Again, Chicago goalie Al Rollins was the victim. The score came in Gordie's 624th NHL contest, and the Wings won the game by a 3–2 count. It was at the Montreal Forum—on December 13, 1958—that Howe notched the 400th goal of his career. Jacques Plante was in the nets. It was Howe's 805th game.

On that 400th goal, by the way, Howe was being checked by Rocket Richard. "I saw someone firing from the outside," Richard recalls somewhat painfully. "Howe reached for the puck.

I lifted his stick off the ice with my stick. The puck hit his stick and went in. I should have gotten an assist on that goal."

Which brings us back to Madison Square Garden on the night of March 14, 1962. It is Howe's 1,045th game. Gump Worsley is in the net for the Rangers. A capacity crowd of 15,925 is on hand.

Each team scores a goal in the first period. Then, early in the second, the Rangers net a second goal and move into the lead. Late in the period, the Wings draw a penalty and Howe takes the ice along with Alex Delvecchio to hold off the Rangers for two minutes.

With a minute gone in the Detroit penalty, Delvecchio intercepts a New York pass at the Detroit blue line. Alex starts up ice with Howe a few strides ahead and to his right. Just as he hits the center line Delvecchio shoots the puck to Gordie a few strides short of the Ranger zone. What Howe does in the next five seconds represents one of the great moments in hockey.

For as Gordie moves across the Ranger blue line, waiting to meet him is Doug Harvey, one of the top defensemen in NHL history. Howe fakes to his right, then swings left, trying to get around Harvey. Harvey hits Howe, and for a split second Gordie loses control of the puck. But somehow, he manages to slide off Harvey's check. Then, Howe reaches out with the stick in his left hand and pushes the puck ahead of him.

The next instant Howe has his right hand on the stick and is around Harvey. Clearly beaten now, Harvey, in a desperation move, trips Howe. As Gordie falls to the ice, he flicks his wrists, and the the puck jumps off his stick and flies under Worsley, who flops to the ice in front of the net —just a split second too late.

Despite Howe's heroic effort, the Wings lose 3 to 2 when New York's Andy Bathgate converts a penalty shot midway in the third period. Still, after the game, most of the talk is about Howe's "impossible" goal. Even old-pro Harvey is philosophical.

"Ordinarily," he says, "I'd feel bad about being faked out. But the big guy has done it before and I'm sure he'll do it again."

Howe added two more goals that season and, as a result, entered the 1962–63 campaign with a total of 502 regular season scores. And as the season got underway, Howe was thirty-four years old, nearer to thirty-five. A national magazine had been approached by a well-known free-lance writer just before the start of the season and offered a story entitled, "Is Gordie Howe Washed Up?" After due consideration, the magazine's editors decided to wait and see if Gordie Howe was indeed washed up before running the story. The editors showed good sense.

Far from being washed up, Howe was about to embark on one of the most satisfying seasons of his long career. Going at top speed for the full 70-game schedule, Howe notched 38 goals and added 48 assists for a total of 86 points—tops in the league. That gave Gordie the scoring title for the fifth time. In addition, he was named winner of the Hart Trophy for the sixth time.

Howe's 38 goals boosted his career total to 540—just four short of the all-time record held by Richard. Back in 1955, when he was trailing Richard in career goals by 144 (407–263), Howe had remarked: "The record is out of my reach unless I get lucky or he breaks a leg. I'll be satisfied if I wind up my career with 400 goals, and even that will take a lot of doing. Catch Richard? It just doesn't seem possible."

In 1955, Howe was twenty-seven years old and in his ninth NHL season. Asked at that time when he would hit the peak of his game, Gordie replied, "Well, I guess the records indicate I have already. So far my best year was 1952–53 when I scored 95 points. That was two years ago and I don't think I'm any better now than I was then."

By the time he retired in 1960, Richard had

pushed his career goal mark to 544. And although Howe never went over 90 points again, after doing it in 1952–53, his steady scoring pace kept him within striking distance of Richard's record. So, as the 1963–64 campaign got underway, Gordie was on the verge of erasing the Rocket's proud mark from the NHL record books.

Howe tied the record on October 27, 1963, in his 1,126th game. Fittingly, it came at the Montreal Forum. And the goalie was Howe's long-time antagonist, Gump Worsley. During the game, which Montreal won 6–4, Howe was limited to two shots by the close checking of Gilles Tremblay. Howe's first shot of the night was a "riser" from out near the blue line that zipped just wide of the right-hand goal post. He got off his second shot at 11:04 of the third period during a Detroit power play.

Bill Gadsby had picked up the disk in the neutral zone and shoveled it ahead to young Bruce MacGregor. As MacGregor skated into Montreal ice he spotted Howe skating on the right wing. Gordie managed to get a stride in front of Tremblay, took MacGregor's perfect feed, and jammed the puck under the sprawling Worsley.

Despite the fact that Howe's goal put him even with Montreal's own Rocket Richard, the Canadien fans jammed into the Forum that night rose as one and accorded Howe a 90-second ovation. Jean Beliveau, the Montreal captain and a great player in his own right, skated over to Howe and congratulated Gordie on behalf of himself and the Canadiens. Later, Beliveau explained:

"The coach [Toe Blake] and I were both thinking the same thing. When he [Blake] nodded, I went over to shake hands with Gordie. No matter what anybody says, I think it was the right thing to do."

And Blake himself added: "They [the Montreal fans] yelled so loud for Howe that for a minute I thought Maurice Richard must have come out of the stands. They haven't cheered that much since the Rocket left."

Actually, the Montreal fans took Howe's accomplishment with a great deal more grace than did Richard. After Howe had scored goal Number 543, Richard had said publicly that his record should be kept on the books with an asterisk next to it since he had established the original mark in just 978 games. Said Richard:

"They should do just like they did with Babe Ruth when Roger Maris hit sixty-one home runs in 162 games. I missed 169 games because of injuries. Howe has been luckier that way. If I hadn't been hurt that often, I would have scored 100 more goals. I never thought Howe was too good a money player. I don't remember him scoring too many winning goals."

What amounted to a Richard plea was quickly rejected by the president of the National Hockey League, Clarence Campbell. "As far as I'm concerned," Campbell said, "Gordie Howe's 545th goal will be the record-breaker. To keep Richard's total there would destroy the image of who the record-holder actually is."

In conjunction with the Campbell statement, an NHL official disclosed that Howe also held the league record for game-winning goals—96. Richard had 83.

Howe took Richard's protestations calmly enough.

"I'll be very proud and happy to top Richard," he remarked. "I used to say I wish he could keep the record because he's such a fabulous individual and a fabulous scorer. Then, after a slight pause, and with just the hint of a smile, Gordie added, "He's got a pretty fair record going for him so I'll just take my time breaking it. The Rocket isn't going to score any more goals."

For a while it appeared that Howe wasn't going to score any more goals either. He failed to net a score in his next five games and the pressure began to build on Howe and his Detroit teammates. In the midst of the Howe goal famine, even coach Sid Abel was moved to remark that "this record of Gordie's is driving us crazy."

"For a few weeks," Abel continued, "it seemed that everybody was concerned about it except Gordie. But now I think it's beginning to get to him."

On the night of November 10th, 1963, Gordie Howe played his 1,132nd game for the Detroit Red Wings. The contest was at Detroit's Olympia. Montreal was the opponent. But Charlie Hodge was the Montreal goalie, having temporarily displaced Worsley in the Canadiens' net.

Howe was on the ice for almost half of the first period—nine minutes and 34 seconds to be precise. He got off three shots, none of them particularly dangerous. By the midway point of the second period the Wings had a 2–0 lead. But Howe was still drawing a blank. Then, at 14 minutes of the second period, center Alex Faulkner of the Wings drew a five-minute major penalty for cutting Montreal center Ralph Backstrom with his stick.

Abel sends out Howe and another wing, Billy McNeill, to kill part of the Faulkner penalty. The crowd groans. The fans want Howe rested for his regular turn and for use on the Detroit power play. But Abel has a 2–0 lead to protect and Howe is the man he wants on ice while the Wings are short-handed.

With approximately 55 seconds gone in the penalty, Montreal lifts the puck deep into Detroit territory. It hits the end boards, but instead of bouncing out near the cage, the disk stops dead. Detroit defenseman Marcel Pronovost reaches the puck first and darts around the Red Wing cage as Howe and McNeill start up ice.

Pronovost slips the puck to Howe at the Detroit blue line and Gordie calls over to McNeill: "Let's get going!"

This means they'll try for a goal instead of just attempting to kill time. Beliveau and All-Star defenseman Jacques Laperriere are back-skating on defense as Howe, McNeill and Bill Gadsby launch their attack. At mid-ice, Howe passes to McNeill, who is between Gordie and Gadsby. McNeill carries across the Montreal blue line, notes that Gadsby on his left is in better position to score, but flips the puck to Howe instead.

Gordie flicks his wrists the moment he feels the puck on his stick. He is about 30 feet from the net. Hodge moves a foot outside of the cage to cut down the angle, leaving a six-inch opening between his left pad and the goal post. Normally, this is an area that can be covered quickly by the goalie. But Howe's shot, about an inch off the ice, travels with such speed that the puck is past Hodge and into the twine before the goaltender can make a move.

As the rubber hits the cords, Howe's stick flies up. He leaps as he rounds the net, then falls to his knees.

"I knew it was in when I let it go," Howe was to say later. "I just wanted to get it in the net and get it over with."

The Olympia explodes in a crescendo of sound. The Red Wings pour over the boards and Faulkner skates out of the penalty box. His teammates surround Howe, pound him on the back, massage his head, shake his hand. In the seventh minute of a 10-minute ovation, Howe skates over to the Detroit bench and hands the puck to Abel. "Boot," he says, "that's the best pain-killer ever invented. I feel 10 pounds lighter."

A minute or so later he skates over to goalie Terry Sawchuk.

"I can start enjoying life again, Uke," Howe says. "Maybe I'll even stop blinking."

The final score is 3 to 0. But no one in the Detroit dressing room really much cares. Howe is being photographed, filmed, taped and congratulated. Beliveau breaks through the crowd and presents Howe with a four-foot portrait, compliments of the Montreal team.

"Hey, Jean," Howe calls to Beliveau, "there's something wrong with this picture. I've got hair."

Howe is handed a telegram from his former coach and mentor, Jack Adams. It reads: "Congratulations! But what took you so long!"

In another corner of the dressing room, Abel is saying, "I'm relieved for his sake that it's over. I'm glad Gordie got it. He's a great player and it was great to see him score the big one the way he did. . . . it was a heck of a shot."

After he is dressed, Howe spends an hour signing autographs outside the Detroit dressing room. Then, by way of celebration, he and his wife and a few friends stop for sandwiches, then drive out to Howe's rink at St. Clair to watch the first freezing.

It is also a big night for a somewhat obscure Billy McNeill. He is immortalized in the record books as the man who set up Howe's record-breaking goal. McNeill played just 15 games for the Red Wings that season. He had one goal for Detroit—and one assist.

* * *

The following day Howe received a telegram of congratulations from Richard. In Montreal, the Rocket remarked to newsmen: "Now he can start playing his regular game and go on to score 600 goals. I knew he would get it [the record]. He's a great player." Then, as an afterthought, Richard added: "How about that! Scoring both goals [numbers 544 and 545] against my old team."

At Detroit's Monday morning practice session, Howe admitted that the pressure had gotten to him. "I feel altogether different," he remarked. "Maybe now I'll stop being so jittery. It got so that the boys on the team stayed away from me. Everybody from the press was following me around and they [his teammates] didn't feel right about barging in. Now that it's over, I hope we [the Wings] can get together again."

They did.

Chapter Ten

As a team, the Wings wound up the 1963–64 campaign in fourth place—but only five points behind league-leading Toronto. In the first round of the Stanley Cup Playoffs that year, the Wings faced Chicago. The Black Hawks had placed three men on the first team of All-Stars—goalie Glenn Hall, defenseman Pierre Pilote, and center Stan Mikita. The Wings had one first-team All-Star, Gordie Howe. And the Hawks, of course, also had the high-scoring Bobby Hull.

The Chicago-Detroit series went seven games. And the Wings won it, with Howe completely outplaying and overshadowing Hull. Then, in the finals, the Wings faced the Maple Leafs.

Toronto won the first game on a goal by Bob Pulford with just two seconds to play. Then, in the second game, Howe set up Larry Jeffrey at 7:52 of the first overtime to square the series at one game apiece. On the winning goal, Howe carried the puck behind the Toronto net and then passed to Jeffrey right in front, who rammed it home. The Leafs and Wings split the next two games. But Detroit won the all-important fifth game by a score of 2 to 1, with Howe netting the first goal.

Following that fifth game, Dick Beddoes, columnist for the Toronto *Globe and Mail,* made these observations:

"Goalie Terry Sawchuk was picked as the first star last night, a selection guaranteed to inspire no quarrels. But the guy who stars whenever he laces on a pair of skates, the one Wing who never moults—he could have been chosen. Which is to say that Gordie Howe played his normal game. Outstanding, superb, and also pretty good.

"Howe's normal game is to take a regular turn on right wing, kill penalties, play the point on the power plays, averaging more than thirty-two minutes a game. He is the complete hockey player, strong and tough. He has the cold executioner's touch when he wants to separate an irritating rival from puck and intellect.

"Howe scored Detroit's first goal and prevented at least two Leaf goals. He steered Bob Pulford off a breakaway attempt in the second period, and dropped to his knees to block an Armstrong try in the third.

"The partisan crowd saluted his check on Pulford with the howls of abuse that frustrated fans reserve for the good ones."

In the dressing room after the game, according to Beddoes' account, Howe was asked by a reporter if he had heard the booing. "If I said I didn't hear it, I'd be lying," Gordie replied.

Did the booing bother him? "If I said I mind," Howe answered, "that would be a lie too."

The series then shifted back to the Motor City and it appeared almost certain that the Wings would win their first Stanley Cup since 1955.

In the sixth game, Howe scored one goal and assisted on another and the Wings held a 3–2 lead after two periods. But the Leafs drew even midway through the third period and the game went into overtime. Detroit opened the overtime period with a quick rush into the Toronto zone. Forward Eddie Joyal fired the disk from just inside the Toronto blue line, but it banged against the post and skittered off to the left side.

The Leafs retrieved and worked back toward the Detroit end. On ice at the time was Toronto defenseman Bobby Baun. He had been carried off on a stretcher midway through the third period with an ankle injury. Later examination showed a bone crack. But he had returned for the overtime, his ankle numbed by a pain-killer.

On the Toronto rush, Baun had stationed himself near the Detroit blue line. The puck was passed to him. He chopped at it with his stick. The puck bounced through a mass of players, hit a Detroit defender, and was deflected past Sawchuk into the Red Wings cage. After that dramatic finish, the seventh game in Toronto was anti-climactic. The Red Wings came up flat. The Leafs were flying—and won the decisive seventh contest by a score of 4 to 0.

"Our losing that Cup series is one of the biggest disappointments I've ever had," Howe says. "That shot by Baun took the steam right out of us and they just played a lot better than we did in the last game.

"That series was something, though," Howe adds. "We had 14 playoff games and we only had two bad ones—the first one in Chicago and the last one in Toronto. We made up for the first one against the Black Hawks. But there weren't any left after the one in Toronto."

Despite Detroit's heartbreaking loss, Howe was by far the individual star of the Stanley Cup series. In the 14 games he had nine goals and 10 assists. Five of the goals and six of the assists were against the Black Hawks. Against Toronto, Howe had four goals and four assists.

At the start of the 1964–65 season, the Red Wings got off fast and took over first place immediately. Hockey experts predicted that the Wings would soon fade. The experts reasoned that the Detroit team carried too many veteran players who would tire and slow down as the season progressed. The reasoning was sound. But the Wings just refused to cooperate.

Instead of fading in the stretch, Howe, Gadsby, Delvecchio, Norm Ullman and the young Detroit goalie, Roger Crozier, grew stronger. As a result, the Wings finished atop the league with 87 points—four more than compiled by second-place Montreal. Howe played in all 70 games and finished the season with 76 points, fashioned on 29 goals and 47 assists. That made him the league's third highest scorer—behind Chicago's Mikita and teammate Ullman.

As the Stanley Cup playoffs got underway, the Wings were favored to win their first championship since 1955. After taking the first two games from the Chicago Black Hawks in the opening round, the Wings looked as safe as money in the bank, but then a Detroit depression set in. Back on home ice, the Hawks won games number three and four. Detroit took the all-important fifth game by a 4–2 count and again appeared in command. But instead of cracking under pressure, the Hawks came back to win the sixth contest by a 4–0 score. Then Chicago wrapped up the series, winning the seventh and final game by a score of 4 to 2. Against the Hawks, Howe was Detroit's second best scorer, notching four goals and two assists for six points. Ullman led the Wings with 10 points.

The next season, Detroit extracted a measure of revenge. Howe came within a whisker of duplicating his performance of the previous campaign, garnering 75 points on 29 goals and 46 assists, and the Wings placed fourth in the league standings. Again Detroit faced Chicago in the opening round of the Stanley Cup. This time the Hawks captured two of the first three games and seemed headed for the Cup finals. But it was Detroit which captured the next three games and the Wings advanced to the finals against Montreal.

Howe & Company extended their Stanley Cup winning streak to five games, beating Montreal 3–2 and 5–2 at the Forum. But again the Stanley Cup eluded the Wings. Holding Detroit to six goals while scoring 14 themselves, the Canadiens swept the next four games and carried home their second consecutive Stanley Cup title. In the 12 Cup games, Howe had six goals and four assists. Only Detroit's Ullman and Delvecchio had more playoff points.

Chapter Eleven

ON THE NIGHT Gordie Howe scored the 545th goal of his career, breaking Richard's record, he said flatly that the National Hockey League mark he coveted above all others was still somewhere in the future.

"Actually," Howe said at the time, "the thing I've wanted most is to play more than 20 seasons in the league."

As Howe skated onto the ice for the first game of the 1966–67 campaign, he achieved that goal. The 1966–67 season was Howe's twenty-first—a record. Dit Clapper of Boston and Howe's one-time teammate, Bill Gadsby, had shared with Gordie the old mark of 20 years in the NHL.

Despite Howe's presence in the lineup, the Wings got off to a miserable start. Even Gordie couldn't get untracked. And by mid-December,

Detroit was mired in last place. It wasn't so much that the Wings had lost their scoring punch. With Howe, Delvecchio, Ullman, Bathgate, Prentice, Henderson, and MacGregor on the forward lines, Detroit still managed to put the puck in the enemy net with a fair degree of regularity. The problem was Detroit's defense—or lack of it.

With Gadsby retired, and with Doug Barkley's career cut short by the tragic loss of an eye, the Wings were all but helpless when it came to defending their goal. At the time of crisis, Sid Abel made a not too surprising decision. He called on Gordie Howe to step into the breach, shifting him from the forward line to defense.

Howe took the change calmly, then threw himself into his new position with the eagerness and dedication of a young rookie trying to make the club for the first time.

On defense, Howe was more than adequate. At times, in fact, his defensive play bordered on the brillant. Which should not have been too shocking. Howe had studied the art of defense, just as he had studied all aspects of the game. In his book, *Hockey-Here's Howe,* Gordie had this to say about the art of playing defense:

"A defenseman must be a specialist at playing the point under conditions where the sides are at equal strength and on the power play. He's expected to kill penalties. He's expected to be sort of a secondary goalkeeper with a knack of dropping into shots.

"He must be a top passer. He has to be better at skating backwards than any other player on the club. He must be prepared to cover up if his forwards are caught up ice. He must be prepared to spend more time on ice than anyone except the goalkeeper. He must be a good checker. And most of all, he must defend."

Howe cites four important rules for a defenseman— (1) Never take your eyes off the play; (2) always stay between the puck carrier and the goal; (3) never get so close to the goaltender that you are a hindrance rather than a help; (4) once you get the puck, get it out of your zone.

Howe also has a tongue-in-cheek comment on what a defenseman should do when caught back in a three-on-one break.

"As Lefty Wilson, our trainer and spare goalkeeper once said," according to Howe, "the best advice I can give is to 'Spread out!' "

He was spotted on defense for a month or so. But he was returned to his slot on right wing after the Wings picked up veteran defenseman Howie Young in mid-season. It was just about that time that the Wings took off on a long winning streak that propelled them from last place to fourth. For a stretch of a dozen games, Detroit was the hottest club in the NHL. And, for a time, it appeared that the Wings would reach the Stanley Cup playoffs in spite of their horrendous start.

But the bubble burst in mid-February during a game against the first-place Black Hawks at the Olympia. Detroit had surged to a 2–0 lead in the first period and seemed to have the game well in hand when Chicago suddenly exploded for three goals within a 10-minute span of the second period. The final score was 3–2 and Detroit was off on a six-game losing streak from which it never recovered.

In analyzing Detroit's collapse, one cannot fault Howe. Despite some torn ligaments in his knee that forced him to miss a greater part of the training season, Gordie still wound up among the top scorers in the league and for the eighteenth consecutive season he notched more than 20 goals. As of the 1967–68 season, Howe had been an All-Star choice 12 seasons in a row. He last failed to make the All-Stars in 1954–55, when he finished third in the voting behind Rocket Richard and Boom Boom Geoffrion. After finishing third in the first-half voting during the 1966–67 season with 25 points, Howe led all right-wingers in the second-half with 71 points.

In late February of 1967, in what has to be the

twilight of his great career, still another well-deserved honor was bestowed on Gordie Howe. At a dinner in New York City, he was presented with the second annual Lester Patrick Award. The award honors the memory of the first man to own a National Hockey League franchise in the United States—the New York Rangers—and is presented for outstanding service to hockey in the United States.

Special guests at the dinner included Howe's "all-opponent" team, plus his "all-star" team of ex-Detroit mates. His all-star club of former team-mates included goalie Harry Lumley, defensemen Bob Goldham and Bill Gadsby, center Sid Abel, and left-winger Ted Lindsay.

Howe's all-opponent team was made up of three former Montreal Canadiens—goalie Bill Durnan, defenseman Doug Harvey, and at the right-wing spot, Rocket Richard. Center Milt Schmidt and defenseman Fern Flaman of the Boston Bruins, plus left-winger Doug Bentley of the Chicago Black Hawks, rounded out Gordie's all-opponent sextet.

The main speaker at the dinner was Howe's first coach and the first winner of the Lester Patrick Award, Jack Adams. In paying tribute to Howe, Adams said:

"This boy is the greatest thing ever to put on

skates. It is an honor to have him follow me as the second winner of this award. If it had not been for Howe, I would not have been the first winner."

Then it was Gordie's turn to speak.

He received a standing ovation from the assembled hockey greats. Then, quietly, he paid tribute to the founding fathers of the NHL—Lester Patrick, Jack Adams, and Conn Smythe of Toronto.

"Thank God for people like this," Howe said. "Where would we be without them?"

Howe went on to say that he was not an emotional-type player on ice; that he was not the type to jump around and wave his stick after scoring a goal. The one time he had jumped into the air, said Howe, was after he had scored the 545th goal of his career. "And that time," Gordie related with a smile, "I fell down."

Finally, Howe remarked that while he might appear outwardly composed, "I'm really nervous as hell." Then, after a pause, he added: "I might not show it. But I'm as tickled as hell inside."

The 1966–67 hockey season ended its regular schedule two days after Howe celebrated his thirty-ninth birthday. But in spite of the advancing years, Howe still intends to continue playing, at least through the 1967–68 campaign.

"I'll be back for sure next year," Gordie commented as he finished out his twenty-first season in the NHL. "I'll leave it up to Sid Abel to tell me when I've reached the end of the line. I'll play next year and then see what Sid thinks. As for retiring, I have no set date. It will be when Sid thinks I'm through and can no longer help the team."

"Gordie will play as long as he enjoys the game," Abel says. "Maybe that will mean two or three more seasons. I don't think I'll have to tell him when he's through. He'll know himself.

"Some day he'll find the injuries and the bruises are too tough and that playing hockey is a chore and no longer fun. Then he'll come to me and say, 'I've had enough.' "

Chapter Twelve

HOCKEY'S most critical observers have unanimously agreed that Gordie Howe has been the closest thing to Superman that ever laced on a pair of skates. Without him, the game might have suffered irreparable damage, for Howe emerged at a time when hockey was entering a period of depression.

Following the bountiful World War II and post-war years, attendance at NHL arenas began to sag in the early fifties. There were rumors that the Boston Bruins franchise—once the strongest in the league—might collapse. But as long as Howe was around there were sure to be crowds, and as long as there were crowds there would be hockey. It would not be at all far-fetched to suggest that Gordie was partially responsible for saving the game in the early fifties.

Ironically, though, Gordie views the situation from another angle. As he sees it, it was hockey that saved him, although it once almost killed him. "If I hadn't come back to hockey," he says, "who knows? I still might be breaking my back paving sidewalks in Saskatoon as I did before I left home to play hockey."

During his more than 20 years in the game Howe has heard his game vilified as being too rough; it has been blasted for its complexity and thoroughly tarred and feathered for an assortment of other so-called weaknesses. And, over these years, nobody has been a more articulate—and sensible—defender of hockey than Howe.

Once, Howe and I sat down together and composed an article called "Nobody Can Knock Hockey To Me" in which the Detroit star explained his views about and defended the game that made him famous. He harked back to the blackest day in his life; that night in March 1950 when he lay in Harper Hospital with a few yards of bandages wrapped around his head and a big, fat patch over his right eye. The delicate three-hour operation had been performed relieving the pressure on his brain. His mother and sister had visited him and he was alone.

"After they left the room," he explained, "I began to think. 'Here I am twenty-two years old and almost ruined for life because of hockey.' My head throbbed like a pneumatic drill. 'Was hockey worth it?' I wondered. It didn't take long for me to answer that. Despite the pain shooting up and down my body, I was eager to get on the ice again. Since the season had ended, I had to wait five long months to find out whether I was capable of a comeback. I spent much of the summer doubting if I could come back.

"Once, while playing baseball, I was pretty much convinced my sports career was behind me. Whenever someone threw the ball shoulder high, I'd see two balls instead of one. Friends said I should lay off hockey, but I had already made up my mind to give it a try. In September, I reported to training camp for my big test.

"When I skated on the ice, I felt a little jittery, but once I made it through the first practice I knew I'd be okay. After a couple of games I felt better than ever and I continued to improve as I went along. I led the NHL in scoring that season for the first time. I knew I had made the right decision in coming back. I knew then and I know now that I owe every good thing I've gotten out of life to hockey."

Howe's critics have charged that he has played the game too rough. Perhaps he has compensated for the damage inflicted upon himself. Perhaps, not. Andy Bathgate, who was Howe's teammate during the 1965–66 and 1966–67 seasons, wrote an article in which he severely castigated hockey for its inherent brutality. Bathgate then was a member of the New York Rangers. Fingered, along with several other NHL stars in the article, was Howe. Bathgate warned that unchecked brutality was going to kill somebody unless something was done about it. He built up spearing as a potential killer and accused a lot of players, including Howe, of playing the game too roughly.

When I discussed the matter with Howe, he accused Bathgate of greatly exaggerating hockey's dangers. "Hockey is the fastest body contact sport in the world and the speed and force of it automatically set up slam-bang situations. When you're skating like a demon and a guy belts you, you don't stop to congratulate him for the lovely check. All you know is that it hurts and you want to retaliate. We can't act like women at an afternoon tea. We must accept roughness as being basic to the sport. Most of the fellows do."

Certainly Howe does. On several occasions during his career, he was badly damaged by Eddie Shack, the runaway truck of the Boston Bruins who has played for the Toronto Maple Leafs and New York Rangers, and whose assignment has been to guard Howe. Once, Shack, travelling at 26 miles per hour, crashed into Howe. The lumber from Shack's stick shaft creased Howe's skull and sent Gordie reeling and bleeding to the ice.

"I can't fault Shack for checking me hard all the time," Howe said. "He's been doing it for years—boarding me, holding me, high-sticking me. After a game against him, fans have asked me, 'How can you stand Shack?' I tell them that Eddie is doing his job and doing it well. I dish it out myself, so I have to be able to take it."

In time, Bathgate apologized to Howe for the allegations made in his article, and Howe accepted the apologies. "I know that down deep hockey means as much to Andy as to the hundreds of players who will defend it any time they're asked. What other sport has such a terrific record of producing successful, happy and wealthy men? Look at the record. Four hockey players—Lionel Conacher, Bucko McDonald, Howie Meeker and Red Kelly—were elected to the Canadian Parliament either during or after their hockey careers. Red Dutton, former defenseman with the New York Americans, became one of the richest men in Canada. Almost every member of the Rangers' Stanley Cup champion team of 1939–40 became either a coach or a manager."

Just as Howe has been willing to take on all opponents on the ice he has been just as willing to face the critics in print. When a list of hockey's "defects" was presented to him, he went over them, one-by-one with me, and supplied the answers. These are the charges and his answers:

Charge: Hockey lacks colorful players and super-stars.

"What about Bobby Hull, Jean Beliveau, Stan Mikita, Frank Mahovlich, Bobby Orr, Bobby Rousseau, Paul Henderson, Norm Ullman, Henri Richard and Roger Crozier?"

Charge: Rules are too complicated.

"Hockey rules are no more complicated than baseball rules. In fact, hockey can be the simplest game in the world to watch. All a fan has to know is that the purpose of the game is to put the puck into the net. As for the red and blue lines, they all have a purpose, the prevention of offsides. It may take a little learning to master line rules but after a few games most fans can figure them out. Even before that, a fan can enjoy the game."

Charge: The Stanley Cup playoff system is illogical.

"Nonsense. What can be more sensible than a system which maintains interest right down to the last day of the season? This is just what the playoff system does. Furthermore, almost every playoff game is a sellout. Why kill the goose that laid the golden egg?"

Charge: The best team doesn't always win the Stanley Cup.

"Take this sampling—from 1955 to 1960 the Montreal Canadiens won the Stanley Cup five times and finished first four out of those five times. The year they finished second, the Canadiens were only three games out of first. I think this indicates that in most cases the best team is the Cup winner."

Charge: NHL owners are only interested in making money.

"Who isn't? But what you don't read about is how much the owners spend on kids' hockey, in promoting the game in local playgrounds. Were it not for the financial support given by NHL teams, thousands of young hockey players would be unable to play, let alone equip themselves for the game. Hockey is an expensive game to operate. I can't blame owners for trying to stay in the black. But hockey gives its money back to the players. Don't forget that the NHL gives every single trophy winner $1,000. Members of the first NHL All-Star teams get $1,000 too. Every member of the first-place team gets $2,250. Second-placers get $1,250 apiece, third, $750 and fourth $250. On top of that the Stanley Cup teams get additional bonuses. Each member of the Cup-winners averages about $3,500 apiece over and above all other bonuses."

Charge: Hockey fights are staged.

"I'd rather not dignify that charge, but let's put it this way: Since body-contact is legal in hockey, a player can get belted more than a dozen times in a game. Unlike football, he doesn't have time to cool off after every play; the action is continuous. Multiply the whacks by 30 players and you have more than 300 collisions in a game. Somebody is bound to get riled under such conditions and, inevitably, a fight will erupt. Actually, hockey doesn't need fights to attract customers. In fact, NHL president Clarence Campbell ordered an investigation a few years ago in the hopes of eliminating some of the fighting."

Charge: The game is too fast.

"We think that's one of hockey's best advertisements—it's the fastest game on earth. There are few lulls because players are permitted to substitute while play continues. That's why you sometimes have action for three to five minutes without a let-up. You get your money's worth at a hockey game. You pay for action and you get it."

Charge: Play is without plan nor purpose.

"Don't be fooled. There is meaning behind every rush. Our club holds practices every day other than the day of a game to perfect plays. We continually plan and refine patterns. Hockey is a very flexible game. Plays don't have to start at the line of scrimmage or when one team loses the ball.

Our plays begin spontaneously and without signal-calling and therefore demand split-second reactions. For example, if the Rangers carry the puck out of their zone and we intercept it, our men instantly have to form a play for an attack on the Ranger goal. There can be a dozen different plays to choose from but one will fit the occasion. Sometimes, because of the speed, play gets a bit scrambled. This is inevitable, considering that the players manipulate the puck with artificial arms (the sticks) and move with artificial legs (the skates) on a slippery, artificial floor (the ice)."

Charge: There are too many ties.

"Football and soccer have ties; why not hockey? With a heavy 74-game schedule it's too much to ask a player to indulge in an overtime period. Then there's often the problem of transportation. Overtime periods would foul up transportation scheduling."

Charge: The schedule is too long.

"Even though the season starts in October and ends in the early spring, fans apparently don't get enough hockey. Attendance keeps climbing. Why shorten a schedule and deprive fans of what they want?"

Charge: Refereeing is inconsistent.

"Hockey is a game of mistakes. Referees are human and just as apt to make mistakes as players.

Except that when a player makes a mistake he can usually count on a teammate to cover up for him. Referees can't. I think a hockey referee has the hardest job of any sports official. He has less than three seconds to whistle down an infraction. With ten players scooting around so fast, it's almost impossible for a referee to detect every infraction and to file mentally through an 85-page rulebook in three seconds to call a penalty. Under the circumstances I think referees do a miraculous job."

Charge: There are too few Americans in pro hockey.

"That's true, but more and more Americans are playing the game and, eventually, there will be more in the NHL. Rinks are shooting up all over the United States. The United States' colleges are taking to the game in a big way and many of the larger American cities are starting kids' hockey programs that we hope will produce NHL players."

Charge: Youngsters are forced to forsake an education to become pro hockey players.

"Hogwash. The Red Wings are willing to send any promising young player in their system to high school or college. Many hockey players such as Red Berenson, Red Hay and Carl Brewer are college graduates. A few years ago, the Chicago Black Hawks not only paid Eric Nesterenko's tuition at the University of Chicago but also flew him to Hawk games when the club played out of town. If a boy prefers to pursue an education before entering pro hockey, he always can go to college where he can study and play hockey."

During our conversations, Howe bridled at the barbs that were mentioned about hockey. The totality of his devotion, respect and joy in the game was summed up in Gordie's sincere explanation:

"How can I sit back and accept any criticism of hockey after all it has done for me? I still can remember back to my childhood, living on our farm in Floral, Saskatchewan, just outside of Saskatoon. On those freezing nights after playing hockey I'd sit in front of the radio, listening to Foster Hewitt broadcast the Toronto games. Sometimes I'd leaf through the Eaton's Department Store catalogue and admire all the gifts. I'd dream of owning them and giving my mother anything she wanted. But we were nine kids in a house without central heating and we certainly weren't rich enough to buy gifts from an Eaton's catalogue.

"I also had some far-out thoughts about becoming a big-league hockey player. I had loved hockey from the first time I put on blades. We'd play in 30- and 40-below weather until we hardly could feel our toes. And when we weren't playing, we'd light matches inside our boots to keep our feet warm. But we loved every minute of it, especially those of us who finally got an invitation from a professional team.

"When my invitation came in August 1943, I attended the Rangers' training camp in Winnipeg and I was a scared fifteen-year-old on his first trip away from home, and I sure was homesick. Finally after ten days the Rangers asked me to play junior hockey for Father Murray's Notre Dame team in Wilcox, Saskatchewan. I was pretty homesick at the time so I said no and went back to Saskatoon.

"The Rangers invited me to camp again the next year but none of the other Saskatoon kids wanted to go. They all were heading for the Red Wing camp so I went with them. Luckily the Wings liked me and Jack Adams signed me to play for Galt, Ontario, in the OHA Junior A League. Only one thing bothered me at the time and Mr. Adams sensed it.

" 'What's the matter, son?' he asked me. 'I won't play for Galt unless I get a bonus,' I said nervously. 'What do you want?' he asked. 'A brand new Red Wing jacket,' I said, as if that was the most important thing in the world. I got it and felt like the richest kid in Canada.

"After you've been around for a while you realize that hockey is more than a fun game and owning a bright red blazer is not the only thing that matters. You soon understand that hockey is your livelihood—and a very lucrative one. I figure that I've collected more than $80,000 in NHL bonuses alone since joining the Wings and that doesn't include my regular salary, special team bonuses or my income from outside interests.

"Then there's the terrific NHL pension plan, the best in sports. When I'm 65 years old, I'll be able to collect about $13,000 a year from the league for the rest of my life. Where can a guy who never had a high-school education get a deal like that?

"Of course, hockey means more to me than dollar signs. A fellow gets great satisfaction in becoming an accomplished athlete. How can a fellow like me express his appreciation for being named for the various honors I've received? How can I tell Jack Adams how much I appreciate what he's done for me—signing me to all those contracts with the Wings, more than any player in the team's history?

"Hockey not only has given me wealth and prestige but also was responsible for my romance. I never would have met my lovely wife, Colleen, were it not for hockey.

"Hockey brought me into contact with business people, too, and got me started in a couple of enterprises with Al Kaline of the Detroit Tigers and Frank Carlin. I almost got into horse racing, too. When I told Jack Adams about that he said: 'Gordie, do anything you want—but just don't ride 'em!'

"Because of hockey I have an income that I never dreamed possible when I was a kid in Saskatoon. I have never forgotten those cold nights when I sat in bed, reading Eaton's catalogue and wishing we were rich. As soon as I was able to, I bought my mother everything she ever had wanted from that catalogue.

"I have been able to provide very well for myself, too. I have a home in Detroit and my family lives in a way I always dreamed they would. A few years ago when we moved into our new house word got around that Gordie Howe was living in the neighborhood. Youngsters began coming to the door where they would ask Colleen: 'Is Gordie Howe here?' If she said I wasn't they'd sometimes peek around her to be sure she was telling the truth.

"When I'm home, I'll either ask the kids in or go out and talk with them. Usually they ask for autographs or for hockey instructions. Once, a bunch of kids came around when I was taking my pre-game nap and Colleen told them I was sleeping, resting up to play. They began telling each other, 'Keep still, Gordie's trying to sleep,' and they made more noise that way than they could have made intentionally.

"The kids and the fans help make the game worthwhile. One game I'll never forget took place on March 2, 1959. The Detroit rooters gave me a 'night' then and I received more than $10,000 worth of gifts. I also had one of the biggest surprises of my life. A station wagon was driven on the ice and inside it were my parents, Mr. and Mrs. Albert Howe. It was the first time my dad had seen me play hockey.

"The fans in Detroit always have been great to me. As you might expect, though, the fans in other cities haven't been as kind. For years I was booed the loudest in Montreal. Every time I stepped on the ice, the French-Canadians would yell: 'Chou Howe, Chou Howe'—Howe, you're a cabbage-head.

"There was good reason for it, of course. The Montreal fans' favorite was Rocket Richard, the great scorer, and since I was the Rocket's closest competitor, the fans would hoot like the devil whenever I took the ice.

"Funny, though, in time a lot of the booing stopped and since then I've felt that many of the Montreal fans have learned to like me. When I was introduced at the NHL All-Star Game in 1960, which was played in Montreal, I received a

15-second standing ovation, and at Christmas, most of the 300 or so cards I received came from Montreal.

"Mind you, not all letters are friendly. Remember the fight I had with Lou Fontinato of the Rangers? Well, after that one, I got some crank letters that were pretty bad. One day, when I returned from practice, Colleen told me she had seen the mail. 'I screened the letters that were the worst and won't let you see them,' she said.

"That made me laugh. 'You screened them,' I said. 'Ha, you should have seen the real nasty ones that I pulled out before I brought that batch home to you.'

"I guess there's still a lot of the small-town farmer in me and I can't deny that I enjoy receiving fan mail and I still get a kick out of being recognized as a celebrity. At one time, there were two cities, New York and Boston, where I could count on walking without being spotted, but not any more.

"Around 1960 an usher stopped me on the way into the Paramount Theater in New York. 'You're Gordie Howe, aren't you?' he said, and he asked for my autograph. Later, I was walking down Broadway with Murray Oliver, who then was my teammate, when two sailors stopped me and introduced themselves.

"I get a kick out of that but I get my biggest kicks from the game itself. For me, one of the top thrills of all wasn't a goal or a Stanley Cup victory but the moment I signed my first NHL contract. That was when my childhood dreams were realized and nothing can ever duplicate it.

"Another thrill I'll never forget was my 325th goal, the one that broke Nels Stewart's record. A third top thrill was the assist I got when I fed Ted Lindsay a pass on the last day of the 1949–50 season to help him win his scoring championship. And, of course, there've been many, many others since then.

"If I had my way, I'd play hockey for the rest of my life but I realize that sooner or later, like Rocket Richard, I'm going to retire. When that day comes I'd like to stay in the game, maybe take up coaching or even refereeing.

"The best way I can express my feelings about hockey is by telling you that I hope my three sons, Marty, Mark and Murray, get into the game. I always felt that I wanted my children to grow up knowing and appreciating what their father does for a living, and, for a while, that posed a problem.

"The older most fathers get, the more established they become in their jobs. When men are forty and fifty, their kids are old enough to grasp their father's importance. But in hockey, you're often 'old' at thirty, and I was beginning to worry that my sons would grow up completely ignorant of what hockey has meant to me and to them.

"But, sometime in 1960, Marty had gone up to his room to go to sleep. I was there tucking him under the covers and he looked up at me, glowing.

" 'Gee, Daddy,' he said. 'Why didn't you tell me you were a famous hockey player?'

"That made me feel good all over."

Chapter Thirteen

WHEN Abel eschewed the Detroit coaching position and presented the job to former defenseman Bill Gadsby at the start of the 1968-69 season, the Howe dilemma was greater than ever. Gordie was now forty years old. To most seasoned observers there appeared to be no way that the man entering middle-age could duplicate his 39 goals and 82 points of the 1967-68 season.

Gadsby, who for years had been Gordie's teammate, underlined the problem very succinctly. "A guy his age," said the rookie coach, "needs his rest the day after a game. Gordie hasn't slowed down so much—he just gets tired easier. After four games in five nights, he might be dragging his rear a bit more."

So when the new season began in October 1968, Gadsby had it all figured out. He'd rest Howe whenever possible; excuse him from strenuous workouts and establish a "laissez-faire" policy which would be governed by the old pro's intuition more than anything. But when Gadsby suggested that Howe limit his workout to 15 minutes, Gordie vetoed the idea.

This was significant. His chronological age notwithstanding, Howe still had the giddiyap of youth. He was on the ice because he *wanted* to be on the ice and the fact that he happened to be forty years old was totally irrelevant. He approached his 23rd season with the élan of a successful young author beginning a new book. "The excitement," said Howe, "is the game itself." But there was more to it than that. In a major deal with the Toronto Maple Leafs, the Red Wings had obtained forwards Frank Mahovlich, Garry Unger and Peter Stemkowski in exchange for Norm Ullman, Floyd Smith and Paul Henderson. Gadsby placed the Gulliver-like Mahovlich on a line with Howe and Alex Delvecchio and soon beautiful things were happening to Howe.

In a way it was almost a "déja-vu" experience for Gordie. A latter-day Production Line had been born and Howe again was to be its balance-wheel. To Howe the difference between Mahovlich and Gordie's former partner on the left, Ted Lindsay, was fascinating.

"The difference," said Howe, "was like night and day. Ted was rambunctious. He'd lay the lumber on everybody. Frank skates for the holes. I've never seen a player who could skate for those holes better, although Ted was pretty good at it. Then there's the difference between being quick and fast. Ted was quick. He was like a quarter horse—a fast starter. Say, take from the net to the blueline, he could beat Frank. But from the net to the far blueline, Frank could beat Ted. Frank is fast."

Mahovlich joined the Red Wings in March 1968 but it was generally acknowledged that he required the final month of the 1967-68 season to accustom himself to his new teammates. Likewise, Howe and Delvecchio required some experimentation to determine how to readjust their styles to that of the Big M.

It was assumed that the Red Wings' ultimate position in the standings would depend upon Howe's position in the scoring list; either high, medium or low. A year earlier Detroit had finished dead last. Now, with Mahovlich and young Unger and Stemkowski, they were considered good enough for better things. The addition of tough Bobby Baun on defense and the vitality of Gadsby behind the bench were also regarded as plus factors in the Wings' favor.

Detroit comported itself respectably through the early weeks of the 1968-69 season and appeared quite capable of making a run on a playoff berth. Once this was established all eyes became riveted on Howe and his newest assault on the record book. This time it was the 700–goal peak, a mountainous climb never before dreamed conquerable; but, then again, nobody ever thought

Gordie was capable of playing 23 consecutive seasons in the NHL and there he was doing it quite well, thank you.

By the beginning of December 1968, Howe had ascended to the point of 699 goals and, once again, the spotlight was trailing him around the league. "They were ready for a big celebration in Olympia Stadium if he got the big goal at home," said Detroit columnist Joe Falls. But Howe and his teammates couldn't untrack themselves before the local fans and on December 4th the Red Wings moved to the cavernous Civic Center rink in Pittsburgh for a game against the Penguins.

Compared with most NHL clubs, the Pittsburgh sextet was less than formidable. Apart from stalwart goalie Les Binkley, the Penguins were a collection of nondescript characters destined to finish out of the playoffs for the second year in a row. As a result, December 4th was regarded as a likely date for Howe to break the record and explained why curator Maurice Reid had flown south from Toronto to collect Howe's stick for display at the Hockey Hall of Fame.

Only seven minutes had elapsed in the first period when Charlie Burns of the Penguins danced his way behind the Pittsburgh net. Mahovlich thrust his blade at the puck and harpooned it away from the Pittsburgh player. Big M skimmed the puck to Delvecchio.

"I didn't even look when I took the pass from

Frank," Delvecchio said later. "I knew Gordie was out there in that general area and I just threw the puck."

Howe was camped approximately 20 feet in front of the Pittsburgh net, somewhat to the left of goalie Binkley. He was being guarded by the veteran defenseman Leo Boivin. The puck moved quickly to Howe. "I didn't have much time to think," he admitted. "As soon as I got it I snapped the puck along the ice."

Boivin moved too late to deflect the puck and Binkley fell to his knees as soon as Howe cranked his stick. "I saw it coming," said Binkley. "I just couldn't get my pad down in time. It was a nice play all the way."

Only 4,414 spectators were in the 12,000-seat building when the red light flashed but, as Joe Falls observed: "They made as much noise as a crowd of 4,414 can make."

To put the goal—and the milestone—in proper perspective one must evaluate it in terms of what other extraordinary players have done. When Howe scored number 700 it put him 155 goals ahead of the previous NHL career scoring record of Maurice "Rocket" Richard, the *retired* Montreal Canadiens ace. Among active players, Howe's closest competition came from Bobby Hull of the Black Hawks and Jean Beliveau of the Canadiens. Both of those players were below 500 goals. Beliveau, in his 16th NHL season, had 443. Hull, in his 12th season, had 430.

On the night of February 6, 1969 the Red Wings were playing host to the Chicago Black Hawks at The Olympia. Some 14,630 fans had jammed the ancient rink. The Wings had lifted themselves into fourth place ahead of Toronto and Chicago and were making a game bid for the playoffs. A victory over Chicago would put them in an even more comfortable position.

As the overhead timer ticked its way past the 12-minute mark, Howe picked up speed near the Chicago blue line. If he was to get any leverage for a shot at goalie Dave Dryden he would first have to contend with defenseman Matt Ravlich.

In a split second he was around Ravlich. His wrists flicked and the puck was speeding toward the target. Dryden's bulky glove went up to intercept the flying rubber but it was too late. The missile had already bypassed his shoulder and sailed into the net for goal number 714. Gordie scored again at 4:22 of the second period and completed the three-goal hat trick at 7:43 of the same period, whereupon the crowd rose as one and tendered him a standing ovation.

It meant only one thing, Howe would have to once again discard any thoughts of retirement.

He realized that sooner or later some writer would declare that "Howe's next milestone will be 750," but Gordie insisted it wouldn't mean that much to him. "I don't have any more targets," he said, "just years. I figure everything in how many years I can play. The records take care of themselves."

A few years ago, observers found it difficult to perceive any real change in Howe's accelerating powers. But in his 23rd season there were faint signs of diminishing returns. He appeared more weary after a strenuous game and occasionally seemed to be straining on the ice.

Maturity is the most accurate reason for many positive changes in Howe. It is reflected in his behavior both on and off the ice. The youth, who once would have played the game for nothing, reportedly received $85,000 for playing with the Red Wings in 1968–69. His business interests continued spreading, too. Late last season it became known that Howe had invested in cattle. He was so serious about it that he bridled one day when manager Abel suggested that he tell a writer "about your cows."

"The word," countered Gordie, "isn't cows. It's cattle! You see, I've gone in for cattle farming. I bought a hundred head of a cattle called Hereford, and I have them placed on the Calderone--Curran Ranches about 100 miles from Detroit. I don't own any part of the ranch, but my cattle are there. And in the summer months I'll spend some time there."

"But, why cattle?" someone wondered.

"Alive," said Howe, betraying his business logic, "they give milk. Dead they give beef."

Howe's sense of humor has always delighted his audiences but it is subtle. Likewise, his hockey style has lacked the flamboyance of a Bobby Hull or Bobby Orr. And Gordie has always been the first to admit it. "I think my own play can be kind of dull," he said. "Not Hull. I admire strength and he's the picture of it when he's coming up the ice in full stride."

Yet, youngsters continued to revere Gordie as he entered his forties. As a result of a poll conducted by *The Canadian* magazine, Howe was voted one of the most popular players by the kids. "I saw some old movies of him and he was great then," wrote 11-year-old Mark Napier of Toronto, reflecting the consensus of opinion, "He's just as good now, I think."

As Howe aged he became more candid in his interviews. It was a manifestation of his self-confidence and security. In March 1969, when an Oakland, California, interviewer asked him about the pressure of big-league hockey, Howe laid it right on the line:

"They (the management) expect you to eat, sleep and live hockey. To me, that's a good way to go crazy. I don't believe in it. For one thing, you have to take care of the body. That is a hockey player's equipment. You keep in shape and you watch your weight. You eat the things you know you should. Take the day of a game. I would love a steak but I have eggs instead. Why? Because I feel I play better with eggs."

There still was reason enough for Howe to be nervous. As the 1968-69 season neared the homestretch, the Red Wings were being sternly challenged for a playoff berth by the Rangers, Maple Leafs and Black Hawks. Even worse, the Howe line was the only one of the Red Wing forward combinations that was producing regularly; but there was no denying that it *was* producing. The big line was fast closing in on the total points record of 226 for a line in one season. Howe helped set the original record in the 70-game 1956-57 season when he was playing on a line with Lindsay and Norm Ullman. In establishing the mark, Gordie had 89 points, Lindsay 85 and Ullman 52.

But now Gordie was making unprecedented strides toward his personal scoring records as he closed in on his 41st birthday. By March he had easily surpassed 30 goals and the most amazed person in the hockey world was Howe, himself. "When the season started," he allowed, "my objective was to score 30 goals. I knew I'd be playing with Frank and Alex and I figured with those two, my chances would be pretty good to hit 30.

"There is pressure, though. Playing with Frank and Alex means that we have to do the scoring. That's the way things have been this year. We have to stir things up. We don't manage to do it all the time, but we have to try. I suppose there is pressure when you look at it that way."

Gadsby's hope was that the youngsters like Stemkowski, Unger and Peter Mahovlich, Frank's kid brother, could provide more scoring balance in the critical days of March but always the burden seemed to tilt to the Howe line, and the grind began to take its toll. The Rangers, who had three well-balanced, if not spectacular, forward units, opened up a decisive lead over the Red Wings and Maple Leafs and appeared almost certain to finish third. Meanwhile, the Black Hawks fell into a serious slump and slid down to the cellar. That left the Leafs and Wings to battle for the remaining berth, fourth place.

"We can still make it," said Howe on March 18, "by winning our own games. We still have two games left with Toronto, home and home. They are 'four-pointers.' We must win both of them."

The decisive contest was March 22 at Maple Leaf Gardens in Toronto. A crowd of 16,485 turned out for the game and they saw the home club run up a 2-0 lead before Mahovlich golfed home a goal late in the second period. But the Leafs scored again in the last period and captured the game, 3-1. Although Detroit still held a mathematical chance for fourth place, the real signs of the Red Wings' ultimate defeat were obvious on the face of the weary Howe. He had pulled the

Detroit machine as far as he could and now he had very little left in him. Veteran writers such as Al Nickleson of *The Toronto Daily Star* ruefully reported the deflation of Howe.

"Gordie," wrote Nickleson, "managed two feeble shots on the Leafs' goal. Frankly, The Great Gordie was beset by weariness, showing his age in the team's third game in four nights. He just wasn't Howe and the team sputtered."

Detroit finished the season in fifth place, making it the third straight year they finished out of the playoff money.

Gordie had no apologies to make. He finished the season with 44 goals and 59 assists for an astonishing total of 103 points, more than he had ever achieved in a single season, even in his halcyon days with Abel and Lindsay. For the second consecutive year he finished third in scoring—this time behind Phil Esposito and Bobby Hull but ahead of the previous year's winner, Stan Mikita.

Paradoxically, the very fact of Howe's genius and durability remained at the core of the Red Wing problem. For years the Detroit brass sought a younger replacement, "a new Howe." Always, there had been hopes. One year Bruce MacGregor would be labelled "The latter-day Gordie." Another year it would be Ed Joyal, or Larry Leffrey or Paul Henderson. It now has become obvious to everyone but those who refuse to accept the fact that there will *never* be another Gordie Howe.

And the Red Wings only hope is that he can somehow stick around for, maybe, another half a decade.

Howe is realist enough to realize he won't be playing for the Red Wings in 1975. The question perplexing many of the great hockey minds remains—will he ultimately turn to coaching?

It was put to Gordie in the last days of 1968-69 and he surprised more than a few people by replying that, no, it wasn't for him.

"I don't see my family for a month and the children all look as though they've grown a foot. They go skiing and then come home and I hear them talk about it. I'm not a part of it. I'm missing this part of their lives. No, I think when I quit as a player I will just take it easy."

Whether he coaches or not there is no evading the fact that hockey will never be quite the same when the big number nine hangs up his skates. But the record book won't let anybody forget him. Most goals, most assists, most points . . . most of everything.

As his teammate, then coach and, finally, manager, nobody appreciated the talents and personality of Gordie Howe more than Sid Abel.

"It's going to be a bad day around here when he quits," Abel lamented, understating the case as much as any man in the hockey world could. "A very bad day."